Fasten Your Seatbelts

BOB WILLIAMS

UPPER OCTAVE

UPPER OCTAVE

First published in Great Britain in 2024 by Upper Octave

Upper Octave Ltd
124 City Road
London EC1V 2NX

ISBN 978-1-9144894-7-1

A CIP catalogue record for this book is available from the British Library.

Typeset in Georgia and Impact.

Contents

Introduction

Some time ago, having received a certain amount of prompting from my colleagues, I wrote a book about my career in aviation. Before starting on the project, I decided to write about my father's aviation career as well as my own. By combining the two, it would cover a long and significant timeframe.

My father joined the Royal Air Force in 1936. I piloted an aircraft for the last time in 2018.

Needless to say, the changes that took place in aviation over that 82 year period were enormous. Having completed the project, I submitted the manuscript to SunRise and was absolutely delighted when they decided to publish it. Following the success of that book, *Born to Fly*, and filled with renewed enthusiasm, I decided to write another. This one would tell of various events and incidents that occurred during our respective careers.

I settled on the title *Fasten Your Seatbelts*, so, assuming you have done that, here goes...

Chapter 1

British South American Airways

My Father joined the Royal Air Force in 1936 and once he had completed his training at RAF Halton, he was assigned to 18 Squadron. He was abroad pretty much for the whole of the Second World War having been posted firstly to northern France and then Africa, Sicily and Italy respectively. Immediately after the war ended, he spent some time at RAF St. Athen as an instructor and then left the service to start a career in civil aviation.

The first airline he worked for was British South American Airways. The British government had recognised a need to establish a regular air service between Britain and South America so the new airline was created. The man put in charge of it was Air Vice Marshall Don Bennett. Bennett was a decorated wartime pilot (CB, CBE, DSO) who had commanded Bomber Command's 'Pathfinder' force.

From the start, it was made clear that the new airline was to operate British aircraft. Because of the very long distances to BSAA's planned destinations, the British aircraft that were available at the time, wouldn't have been at the top of anyone's shopping list.

The Avro Lancastrian was developed from the Lancaster bomber. It was powered by four Rolls Royce Merlin engines and had a still air range of around 3,500 nautical miles flying at a speed of 200 knots. However, it carried just 13 passengers in its very noisy unpressurised passenger cabin.

The Avro York was also developed from the Lancaster bomber. With a box fuselage, it shared the same wing, undercarriage and Merlin engines as the Lancaster. It also had the same tailplane, but with an additional central vertical fin to improve yaw control. It had a cruising speed of around 200 knots and a still air range of 2,500 nautical miles. It too was unpressurised, so was forced to fly at low altitude through the bad weather rather than above it. With a crew of four, it was configured to carry 21 passengers.

The relatively slow, noisy and unpressurised Lancastrians and Yorks would be at the very limit of their range capability flying to BSAA's far off destinations. A third aircraft type that was added to BSAA's fleet was the Avro Tudor, which was Britain's first pressurised passenger aircraft. Unfortunately, early test flights had shown that the aircraft's performance was sadly deficient. So much so that the Tudor had actually been rejected by BOAC. Despite this fact, whether they liked it or not, these were the aircraft types that BSAA would be using.

Air Vice Marshal Don Bennett was a decorated War hero. Determined and goal-driven were the positive characteristics with which he was often associated. Stubborn, abrasive and short tempered were some of the less desirable characteristics that sprang to mind for many people when his name was mentioned.

With a reputation for straight talking, he was never afraid to air his views forcibly and wasn't interested in winning any popularity contests.

His qualities as an extremely skillful pilot and outstanding navigator were undisputed. However, that didn't alter the fact that he was a difficult man to get along with.

The airport now known as London Heathrow, was formerly known quite simply as London Airport (or LAP for short). It officially opened on the 31st May 1946, however in January of that same year, Bennett wanted to operate the first of a series of proving flights for British South American Airways from the U.K. to South America.

Construction workers were still building the runway at London airport. A collection of bell tents and caravans were littered about the place and the yet to be completed control tower was the only brick building. Bennett wasn't about to let that stop him. He somehow persuaded the construction workers to clear all their plant equipment and vehicles out of the way so that he could takeoff. On the 6th of January 1946 BSAA's Avro Lancastrian took off from London airport five months before the place officially opened!

That flight was also a good example of Bennett's stamina and his determination to keep going until the job was done. He took off at the aircraft controls with Captain Robert Alabaster alongside him. Marie Guthrie was the stewardess looking after the eleven passengers. They routed via Lisbon, Bathurst (now known as Banjul in The Gambia), Natal, Rio de Janeiro and Montevideo. The flight took 36 hours in total and the same crew remained on duty throughout.

Bennett was known for taking short in-flight naps whilst the other pilot minded the shop. He would then wake up refreshed and ready to continue indefinitely. Unfortunately for the rest of the crew, he expected them to be able to keep going indefinitely too. He was a hard man to keep up with.

The short time during which British South American Airways was operational (1946 to 1949) was an incredibly eventful period. In today's World of safe air travel, BSAA's accident record makes horrifying reading. However, we have to understand a number of things:

- They began operating immediately after the Second World War.
- They were flying aircraft that were effectively converted or modified WW2 bombers.
- They were flying long trans oceanic routes that presented enormous challenges in terms of navigation (out of range of all land based navigational aids).
- The aircraft were being taken to the extreme limit of their range capabilities, particularly when flying westbound against the prevailing winds. Needless to say, running out of fuel on a trans oceanic flight is never going to end well!
- The pilots had previously been flying combat operations during World War Two. During that time, they had accepted danger as being a normal part of everyday life. It might be argued that having survived the war, they were now somewhat numbed by living with danger and considered 'Pushing their luck' to be an accepted part of the job.

The shocking fact is, over a period of just 29 months, BSAA suffered 10 crashes.

1. Their first accident occurred in August 1946 when a Lancastrian (G-AGWJ) came off the runway whilst trying to land at Bathurst (now Banjul) in the Gambia.The aircraft was written off.

2. Just eight days later, one of their Avro York aircraft (G-AHEW) was to fly from Banjul to Natal. Soon after takeoff, it crashed killing all 24 people aboard.

3. Seven months passed before, on 13th April 1947, another York (G-AHEZ) tried to land at Dakar in conditions of extremely poor visibility. It made repeated attempts and on it's third attempt to get in, it crashed killing 6 of the 15 people aboard.

4. On the 2nd August 1947, Lancastrian (G-AGWH) was flying from Buenos Aires to Santiago but crashed into the Andes mountain range. An extensive search over many days failed to find any wreckage. Incredibly, 51 years later (in 1998) glacial action in the region disgorged the wreckage lower down the mountain where it was discovered by climbers.

5. A month later, 5th September 1947, Lancastrian (G-AGWK) held over the island of Bermuda for 90 minutes waiting for a severe thunderstorm to clear the area. Then, with no change in the weather but running out of fuel, they attempted a landing. The aircraft came off the runway and was written off. Fortunately, there were no fatalities amongst the 20 people aboard.

6. In the following month, 23rd October 1947, Lancastrian, G-AGWL ground looped attempting to land in a cross wind at London airport. The aircraft was written off, but with

no fatalities. (An aircraft is said to ground loop when it yaws out of control and the tail of the aircraft swings horizontally through 180 degrees, rather like a car performing a handbrake turn.)

7. The following month, on the 13th November 1947, a Lancastrian (G-AGWG) was climbing out from Bermuda on it's flight to the Azores, when it's number four engine caught fire.They declared an emergency and elected to return to Bermuda. During the subsequent approach and landing, the aircraft undershot the runway and was written off. There were no fatalities amongst the 16 people aboard.

8. Two months later on the 30th January 1948, an Avro Tudor (G-AHNP) flying from the Azores to Bermuda disappeared and no wreckage was found. There were 31 people aboard.

9. On 5th January 1949 Avro York (G-AHEX) suffered a tyre failure on takeoff . All appeared to be okay, so it continued towards it's destination. However, the oil system had been damaged and all contents were lost. The number three engine then failed, but they were unable to feather the propellor so the engine broke up and caught fire. The pilots made an emergency spiral descent with the engine fire raging uncontrollably. They crash landed near Caravelas bay in Brazil. There were 3 fatalities amongst the 15 people on board.

10. On 17th January 1949: Tudor (G-AGRE) was flying from Bermuda to Jamaica but disappeared without trace. There were 20 people on board.

A horrific list of accidents over an incredibly short period of time.

The Avro Tudor featured in some of those accidents and ironically, that was the very aircraft type that was supposed to be BSAA's saviour. Britain's first pressurised airliner was powered by four Rolls Royce Merlin engines and with a maximum takeoff weight of 34,500 kgs, it was supposed to be able to carry 24 passengers at 240 knots, over a range of 3,100 nautical miles and to be capable of flying at high altitude above the worst of the weather.

On the strength of these proud boasts, BOAC ordered 18 Tudor 1 aircraft. Sadly, after early trials, the airline was so unimpressed that they ordered over 300 modifications to the existing design. Some of these were far from insignificant, such as the need to fit a much enlarged tail fin to overcome severe directional control deficiencies.

Avro carried out all the requested modifications, but when the aircraft was sent on 'hot and high trials' (operating from airports located significantly above sea level and with high ambient temperatures) it failed to reach the required performance standards. Consequently, BOAC cancelled their order for all the Avro Tudors.

The aircraft that BSAA were given were known as the Tudor 4. These aircraft were stretched (lengthened) versions of the Tudor 1 that BOAC had rejected and had been modified and improved in a number of different ways.

All the BSAA aircraft were given names that included the word Star. For example there was *Star Dust, Star Trail, Star Ariel, Star Tiger* and so on. The stewardesses were known as 'Star girls' one of whom incidentally was the Mother of the entrepreneur Richard Branson.

With the introduction of the new Avro Tudor, the airline started to promote the fact that passengers would be travelling in pressurised comfort and luxury. Needless to say, the travelling public were blissfully unaware of the Tudor's former performance issues and BSAA certainly weren't about to highlight those.

On the 30th September 1947, Don Bennett operated a proving flight from London to Buenos Aires in a Tudor 4 and a regular weekly service began immediately afterwards.

Four months later (30th January 1948) a BSAA Tudor disappeared flying from the Azores to Bermuda. The British air ministry revoked the type's certificate of airworthiness (C of A) pending an investigation.

Questions had been asked in the House of Commons regarding BSAA's accident record, but Bennett, as ebullient as ever, stated that the accidents were to be expected on such challenging routes. Furthermore, he objected to the judicial enquiry into the loss of the Tudor *Star Tiger* because he maintained that a well known wartime saboteur had been spotted near the aircraft just before it set off on it's fatal flight. He also claimed that the British Prime minister, Clement Attlee, had ordered that this line of enquiry should be abandoned. Shortly after this, Bennett resigned from the company. In actual fact, his very public criticisms, along with his refusal to apologise or back down had been the last straw as far as the company was concerned, so his resignation almost certainly preceded a dismissal and they were glad to see him go.

He was replaced by Air Commodore Herbert Brackley. Surprisingly, despite continued concerns, the Tudors were again certified to carry passengers in April 1948 and then two months later, the airline had a slice of good fortune: the Berlin Airlift.

At the end of the Second World War, the city of Berlin had been divided into sectors, each of which was overseen by one of the Allies. There was an airfield in each sector. Gatow in the British sector, Tempelhof in the American sector, Tegel in the French sector. The airfield of Schoenefeld was located within Soviet held territory to the south east of the city.

Britain, America and France knew that this arrangement couldn't continue indefinitely and that steps should be taken to stabilise the ruined German economy. The Russians were vehemently opposed to this idea, but the Western Allies began planning for the creation of an independent democratic west German republic. When the Russians got wind of this, their representative of the Allied control council demanded to see details of the plan. When the western allies refused, the Soviet representative stormed out of the meeting and what became known as the 'Cold War' began in earnest.

Soon afterwards, Soviet military forces began to carry out intermittent stop and search operations, seriously disrupting the traffic bringing supplies into Berlin. The city was totally dependent upon the free flow of these supplies which included food, medicines, oil and coal for heating, in fact everything that is needed for a city to survive. It was normally brought in by road, rail and on canal barges, but now the Soviets were beginning to seriously delay these supplies. On the 24th June 1948, the Soviets blockaded all access routes into Berlin.

The western allies demanded that the blockade should be removed immediately, but to no avail. The city of Berlin and it's inhabitants were seemingly at the mercy of the Soviets.

Under the Allied control council agreement of 1945, the Western allies had guaranteed access to Berlin via three air corridors that linked the city to Western sectors of Germany.

Under the agreement, allied aircraft could fly along these 20 mile wide corridors at any altitude up to 10,000 feet without any need to advise the Soviets. With these three air corridors now providing the only possible access to Berlin, the western allies decided to begin relief flights to the beleaguered city

The US Air Force began operations on 26th June and the British Royal Air Force began on 28th June. The Soviets, convinced that it would be impossible to supply the city by air alone, maintained the blockade in the belief that the Western powers would soon give up. What followed, was the most intensive air relief operation ever carried out. However, it was soon realised that many more aircraft were going to be needed. Consequently, on the 4th August, the civil airlift began and numerous civilian aircraft operators added their weight to the operation.

Over the following ten months, British and American aircraft completed a total of 195,530 flights and on average brought in close to 5,000 tonnes of supplies per day to the city of Berlin.

It was an incredibly well orchestrated operation that required unprecedented timing and navigational accuracy from the participating crews. Day and night, in all weather conditions, aircraft were flying in and out of Berlin at the rate of one every 30 seconds.

Inevitably, with such a demanding operation, there were crashes. Seventeen American aircraft and eight British aircraft crashed, resulting in a total of

101 fatalities. Finally, the Soviets realised that their blockade had failed and on 12th May 1949, the surface blockade was lifted. The relief flights continued for a while in order to bolster reserve supplies at the city in case the Soviets decided to change their mind. On 30th September 1949, the airlift finally ended.

A number of the civilian operators who took part in the airlift made a lot of money and gained a great deal of flying experience in a very short time. At the end of the war, lots of World War Two aircraft had been on offer at knockdown prices due to them being surplus to military requirements. Many were bought by scrap dealers and disposed of, but some entrepreneurs bought ex military bombers and converted them to carry cargo instead of bombs. These aircraft were then quickly pressed into service on the airlift.

The more trips they flew, the more money their owners made, so they flew them around the clock. Aviation entrepreneurs such as Freddie Laker (Aviation Traders) & Harold Bamberg (Eagle) began their airlines in this way.

For British South American Airways, the Berlin airlift proved to be a welcome, albeit temporary Godsend. They bought the Tudor 1 aircraft that BOAC had rejected, plus some Tudor 5s and then operated them very successfully on the airlift, without any accidents.

One interesting and hair-raising incident that occurred during the Berlin airlift involved Air Vice Marshall Don Bennett. At the start of the airlift, Bennett had formed his own company called Airflight Ltd, operating two Avro Tudors.

He had flown one of his Tudors from Wunsdorf to Berlin Gatow and had been cracking the whip to ensure the aircraft was refuelled and turned around as quickly as possible for the flight back out of there. In the rush to get away, he had failed to notice that the elevator control locks had not been removed. These were devices that were physically clamped onto the elevators to hold them firmly in the 'neutral' position so that in gusty conditions when the aircraft was parked on the ground, the elevators could not be moved (and damaged) by the wind. Obviously these should have been removed before starting up and taxiing out for take off, but in his hurry to get away and start another revenue earning flight, they had been overlooked.

The aircraft began it's takeoff and, when it was already going too fast to be able to stop without running off the end of the runway, Bennett realised that the elevators were locked and immovable. By now the end of the runway was rapidly approaching and, with remarkable presence of mind, he quickly spun the elevator trim wheel. This operated the trim tab that was attached to the trailing edge of the elevator and it was still capable of moving freely. He had to remember to operate it in the reverse sense, because normally a pilot would move the trim tab down in order to assist the elevator in moving up. Now with jammed elevators, he worked on the assumption that the tab had sufficient authority to act like a miniature elevator and by moving the trim wheel forward it would make the aircraft go up. His assumption was correct and the aircraft staggered into the air just before the end of the runway.

Now, using the trim wheel for 'back to front' pitch control, he flew the aircraft around the airfield circuit and came back in to land. Exiting the aircraft and removing the external control locks, he then lined up onto the runway and took off again.

This incident clearly demonstrated his ability to think calmly and quickly when faced with an emergency situation. It obviously demonstrated his remarkable stick and rudder flying skills. It also demonstrated that he needed to improve his pre-flight inspection checks and his check for full and free movement of the flight controls prior to starting the takeoff run! Handling skills: 10/10. Preflight checks: 0/10.

When Bennett decided to start his own airline (Airflight Ltd.) he approached my Father saying that he wanted him to leave BSAA and join him. Although many people found Bennett extremely difficult to get on with, he and my Father enjoyed a good working relationship. Consequently, Dad left BSAA and joined Airflight. Following the Berlin airlift, Bennett's Tudors carried out trooping flights for the British government and numerous ad hoc charters under the trade name of 'Fairflight.'

Incidentally, BSAA's successful and accident free run during the Berlin airlift couldn't prevent the company's demise. In January 1949, one of their aircraft (a Tudor 4) had disappeared over the Atlantic with the loss of 20 lives. Following this, all Tudor 1s and 4s were once again grounded by the air ministry. Finally, when in March the company's accounts were published, they showed a substantial operating loss. It was time to throw the towel in and wind up the whole operation.

In July 1949, under the terms of the Airways Corporation act, BOAC took over all the assets and liabilities of BSAA. They immediately introduced new aircraft types (Argonauts and Constellations) which were far better suited to the long distance destinations that BSAA had been serving. The story of British South American Airways finally ended. As stated previously, my Father had joined forces with Air Vice Marshal Don Bennett, who had formed his own airline, operating two Avro Tudor Vs. These very hard working aircraft had operated numerous relief flights on the Berlin airlift, trooping flights on behalf of the British government and many ad hoc charter flights to far flung destinations.

In 1951, one notable trip on which my Father was a crew member started off from Blackbushe airport in Hampshire. The Tudor 5 was crammed full with mailbags to be delivered to the U.S military personnel who were fighting the war in Korea. They were to take the mail as far as Japan and the U.S military would take it on from there. Bennett was determined to get the consignment to Japan in record time and my father knew that meant he was in for an exhausting journey. Little did he realise just how exhausting.

Today, there are strict rules and restrictions with regards to how many hours flight crews can remain on duty. There are also maximum limits on how many flying hours they can clock up in a month or year. In 1951 when they set off on their mail flight to Japan, there were no such restrictions on aircrew flying limits. Bennett was about to demonstrate that in the most dramatic way.

The route the aircraft took for the trip was as follows: Blackbushe - Rome - Athens - Damascus - Bahrain - Karachi - Delhi - Calcutta - Bangkok - Saigon - Manila - Okinawa - Iwakuni. Having reached their destination and unloaded their cargo of mail, they then took the following route back home: Iwakuni - Hong Kong - Rangoon - Calcutta - Karachi - Bahrain - Nicosia - Rome - Blackbushe.

The whole trip was completed by a single crew and

they arrived back at Blackbushe 7 days and 3 hours after leaving. They had completed 130 flying hours, averaging over 18 hours airborne time, every day for a week. Years later, my Mother told me that Dad was so tired when he landed back at Blackbushe, he couldn't even speak properly.

To put it into context, they had completed 130 flying hours in a week. Today, pilots are limited to a maximum of 100 flying hours in a month.

Chapter 2

Freddie Laker

In late 1951, Bennett sold his airline to a British entrepreneur who would soon go on to become very famous in aviation circles. That man was Freddie Laker; a remarkable person. Born in 1922, he had come from a humble background and became fascinated by aviation from an early age. At the age of 16, he joined the aircraft manufacturing company Short Brothers as an engineering apprentice.

Then, in 1940 he joined the ATA as a flight engineer. The ATA (Air Transport Auxiliary) were tasked with ferrying new and repaired military aircraft to the various airfields and units where they were needed.

Having been discharged from the ATA in 1946, he briefly joined British European Airways, but left after a few months claiming that the company left him feeling unchallenged.

He joined London Aero & Motor Services as a flight engineer on their fleet of Handley Page Haltons. These were civilianised Halifax bombers that had been modified to carry cargo. Less than a year later, he left to set up his own company. He named the company Aviation Traders.

Immediately after the end of the Second World War, the military started disposing of their surplus equipment. Incredible though it seems now, at one time local scrap dealers were able to buy a Spitfire fighter for as little as £25 and then cart it off to be stripped and scrapped for whatever profit they could make.

Freddie took full advantage of this bargain basement opportunity and bought a huge assortment of ex military vehicles, aircraft flight instruments, radios, electrical generators, hydraulic pumps and engines.

Over a period of time, Aviation Traders held the largest collection of aircraft spares in Europe. Freddie then bought 10 Handley Page Halton aircraft, with the intention of sprucing them up and selling them on at a profit. However, something changed his plan. The Berlin Airlift.

It soon became apparent to the military powers that were engaged in the airlift that they simply didn't have enough aircraft to do the job. Consequently, they began chartering as many civilian aircraft as they could get their hands on. Of the nearly 700 aircraft that were engaged in the airlift, over a 100 of them were owned by civilian operators. Freddie's Haltons, backed by his considerable spares holding flew around the clock earning Aviation Traders a great deal of money in a short space of time. The company also provided spares and maintenance assistance for many other airlines during that period which brought in even more revenue.

Aviation Traders had made so much money in this way, that it presented Laker with a huge tax bill. To offset this, he bought Air Charter, a company that had been struggling for some time and had run up considerable losses. Freddie used those losses to offset his other company's profit, thereby reducing his tax bill.

At the end of 1951 he purchased Don Bennett's airline, Fairflight, along with all it's employees, my Father amongst them. He combined the airlines into one, calling it Air Charter Ltd. Now, Laker owned an aircraft spares and maintenance company and an airline with a fleet of Avro Tudors, Avro Yorks and Douglas DC-3s. At this stage, Laker was still only 29 years old.

The main reason he had bought Fairflight was because that airline had a lucrative contract carrying cargo between Berlin and Hamburg and now, the second Berlin airlift had begun. With the Russians preventing goods from leaving Berlin and raw materials from getting in by surface transport, the game was on once again for moving it all by air. Eventually, Freddie's airline, Air Charter, was operating more than 70 flights a week between Berlin, Hannover and Hamburg.

In the 1945 general election at the end of the war, the Labour Party had won a landslide victory. Their conviction that all key industries should be state run, meant that they started to nationalise everything in sight: electricity, gas, steel production, road, rail and air transport, all came under the control of the government. In the case of air transport, BOAC & BEA were totally shielded from any competition on their scheduled routes.

In the meantime, none of the independent airlines were allowed a look in. They were trying to survive on ad hoc charters. Following the 1951 general election, the Conservative party was returned to power and they favoured a mixture of public and private sectors in the aviation industry. Whilst they didn't want to alter the secure status of the two state run airlines, they did want to help the struggling independents.

At this time, the British armed forces held Garrisons in a number of overseas locations. Troop movements were required to and from those far flung places and RAF Transport Command didn't have enough aircraft for the job. This became the lifeline that the Conservative government offered to Britain's independent airlines: trooping contracts.

The bidding for those contracts was fierce. At first it was largely cost driven and rival airlines tried to undercut one another, but it wasn't long before they started to gain a reputation for poor reliability and timekeeping. Then, the disappearance of a Skyways York over the Atlantic, with the loss of all the troops and their families on board, prompted questions about safety too.

Never one to miss an opportunity, Freddie Laker approached the authorities with a cunning plan. He knew that there were contracts to be won flying troops to Singapore and onwards to Australia and Fiji. The question was, how was he to convince people that his airline was the best one for the job? His solution was a stroke of genius.

He fitted an Avro York with rearward facing passenger seats, a configuration that he knew won favour with the Military on safety grounds. He also had the passenger cabin lined with soundproofing material in order to reduce noise levels and increase comfort within the cabin. Lastly and most importantly, with Aviation Traders vast supply of aircraft spares at his disposal (which included literally hundreds of Rolls Royce Merlin engines) he promised to set up stores of aircraft parts at strategic locations along the proposed air route. That way, if any of his aircraft developed a technical problem, they could land at the nearest airfield with spares on site and then be quickly on their way again once remedial maintenance work had been completed. Not surprisingly, following this innovative proposal, Freddie Laker won the contract.

In September 1953, Laker bought 10 Avro Tudors that had become available at a bargain price. His intention was to extensively modify each one in the hope that this would result in the Tudor regaining it's unrestricted passenger carrying Certificate of Airworthiness. He then bought all the unserviceable Tudors on the British register, in order to break them down for use as spare parts.

One important aim for the very extensive modification programme, was to significantly reduce the weight of the aircraft and improve it's performance in terms of range and payload carrying ability. All unnecessary equipment was ripped out, including the cabin pressurisation system. The fuel burning combustion heater for the cabin had originally been located in the vicinity of the aircraft's hydraulic system. Crews had long considered this to be a crazy design feature and an obvious fire risk. Indeed some of them crossed their fingers for luck every time they ignited the heater in flight. Now, the whole system was ripped out and replaced by a much lighter system that incorporated electric heating elements. All the aircraft's electrical systems and radio equipment got relocated well away from the hydraulic tank and it's associated components in order to again reduce fire risk. Rearward facing passenger seats were fitted in the interest of improving passenger safety.

The weight reduction programme successfully

reduced the empty weight of each aircraft by approximately 1,000 kilograms . This ensured that a significantly greater payload could be carried whilst still remaining below the maximum takeoff weight. A full Certificate of Airworthiness air test was to be carried out on each aircraft following it's modification and this included stall tests, engine out performance checks and extreme handling manoeuvres. A number of test flights were carried out with the chief pilot of the Air Registration Board (the forerunner of the Civil Aviation Authority). These included long distance flights to determine the effective range and endurance of the aircraft with varying payloads. The result of these test flights exceeded expectations and showed that the Tudor, whilst carrying 42 troops and all their equipment, had an endurance of well over 10 hours at a cruising speed of 185 knots. Furthermore, its takeoff and climb performance figures showed that it could now meet the 1951 British Airworthiness Requirements, which were even more stringent than the BARs under which the aircraft type had originally been certified. Consequently, the authorities now reissued a full unrestricted passenger carrying Certificate of Airworthiness for the Tudor.

Laker knew that he now had a fleet of aircraft that had a range and weight carrying ability that was comparable to a number of more modern types. However, because of the Tudor's low purchase cost, his overall operating costs were also low. That put him in a very strong position against his competitors. He was now a force to be reckoned with.

Everyone now hoped that the chequered history of the Avro Tudor was old news and that Freddie's trust in the type would prove to be justified.

In April 1954, that hope was seriously challenged

when one of Laker's Tudors was flying over central France. The aircraft was at 10,000 feet and flying in cloud with the autopilot engaged. Captain Carreras noted that the airspeed was lower than he would have expected at the current weight and power setting. Suspecting that the aircraft controls might need to be re-trimmed, he placed his hands onto the control wheel and disengaged the autopilot. All Hell broke loose. The aircraft yawed and then banked violently over onto a wingtip, following which it went into a steep spiral dive.

The aircraft lost seven thousand feet in altitude before Carreras was able to regain control and pull out of the dive. When they eventually landed, there were signs of wrinkling on the wings and fuselage that clearly showed the aircraft had been over stressed during the recovery from it's near fatal dive. It had been a very close call.

Knowing that the Aviation authorities and the general public would be demanding answers and also, that the Tudor might once again lose it's Certificate of Airworthiness, Laker instructed two of his senior pilots to immediately begin test flights in his Tudors to try and establish the cause of the incident.

Captain Norman Jennings was the Chief Pilot of Aviation Traders. Captain Mike Davison was their Chief Training Captain. These two individuals, along with Captain Carreras (from the ill fated flight) carried out an intensive series of test flights during which they tried to replicate the high speed spiral dive manoeuvre that had occurred over central France.

They succeeded. Not only that, but they discovered exactly what had caused the aircraft to act in that way. Carreras' aircraft had been flying in cloud and it's Merlin engines had started to experience carburettor icing. Carburettor icing can occur under certain conditions even when the outside temperature is well above freezing and this was the case here. The ice built up more quickly in one of the aircraft's outboard engines, resulting in a subtle reduction in power from that engine. Of course this meant that the combined power of the engines on one wing was greater than on the opposite wing. Because of this asymmetric thrust, the autopilot had difficulty in keeping the aircraft on a constant heading and started to apply a correction to the flight controls. When Carreras disengaged the autopilot, the aircraft was hopelessly out of trim. Before he knew what was happening, it yawed violently which had the secondary effect of rolling the aircraft steeply over into a spiral dive.

To everyone's relief, it was concluded that the aircraft hadn't been to blame. It was obvious that if the pilot had been more vigilant, and had exercised better engine management then the incident would not have occurred. The pilot's operating manual was immediately updated to highlight the problem and detail the techniques to be employed when operating the engines in icing conditions

Laker being the great opportunist, wasn't going to miss the chance to publicise his company's efforts and the importance of their findings.

I have a copy of a notice that he sent to all news editors that makes very interesting reading. It is dated 07th May 1954 and begins 'Not for publication until Monday 10th May.' It then continues:

Sunday 09th May at 3:00 pm, Stansted airport, Essex. # Fatal aircraft crash manoeuvre to be simulated.

Dive 'out of control' from 10,000 feet to 4,000 feet.

British investigators discover the reason for mountain crash.

Press invited to participate & fly in the demonstration aircraft. # Interviews with pilots and photographs available.

Possibly the most important piece of recent British aircraft detective work will be, demonstrated at 3pm Sunday afternoon at Stansted airport. Captain M. M. Davison of Aviation Traders will fly a Tudor aircraft to 10,000 feet and put it into an asymmetric dive of 6,000 feet. He will simulate the incident which occurred to a Tudor south of Paris a month ago, when at 10,000 feet the aircraft went into a sudden dive of 7,000 feet. This manoeuvre, experts say has undoubtedly caused the loss of many passenger aircraft, both British and American, plunging into mountains in bad weather. Until now, the cause of these accidents has never been determined.

Following exhaustive tests since the Tudor incident south of Paris, it can now be authoritatively stated that given certain adverse weather conditions and flying on automatic pilot, aircraft at any height will go into a steep, uncontrolled dive. This can now be rectified with a new set of pilot operating instructions.

Full technical and general details will be released at Stansted on Sunday afternoon by F. A. Laker, head of Aviation Traders. Press are invited to go on the demonstration flight participating in what before has almost always been a disastrous accident.

This manoeuvre has now been safely and successfully completed by Aviation Traders on both British and American aircraft a number of times. Captain Davison is chief training pilot of Aviation Traders. The aircraft used for the demonstration is Tudor 'Roger George' which, two hours afterwards will takeoff for Saigon, carrying medical supplies to the French forces in Indo-China. The aircraft has a full Certificate of Airworthiness for passengers and each press passenger will be covered by insurance up to £10,000.

On Sunday, 9th May 1954, Aviation Traders issued the following notice:

It will be recalled that a Tudor aircraft G-AGRI carrying freight, flown by Captain J. M. Carreras, went out of control in cloud while flying about 10,000 feet above central France and lost a considerable amount of height before control was regained. At the time, the aircraft was being flown by the automatic pilot. Immediately prior to the occurrence the Captain noticed that the aircraft had lost rather a lot of speed and the automatic pilot did not appear to be working correctly. He cut off the automatic pilot prior to flying the aircraft manually and, as it was cut off, the aircraft went into a steep spiral dive. There was some superficial damage on the underside of the main planes due to the high force of 'G' encountered as the aircraft came out of the dive. The damage was not serious and the aircraft went on quite normally to Malta without the crew being aware of it.

The analysis of the evidence given by the crew and of the number of discussions which have taken place between the Air Registration Board, the accidents investigation branch, the manufacturers and the owners, establish beyond any doubt that the aircraft was in an asymmetric condition.

The main trials which have enabled this positive conclusion to be reached were initiated by the owners of the aircraft, Messrs. Aviation Traders Ltd. and carried out by their Training Captain M. M. Davison and by their chief pilot and operations manager Captain E. N. Jennings, flying independently in two different Tudor aircraft. They flew under conditions as near as possible the same as those under which Captain Carreras was flying when his original incident occurred. That is, the aircraft were loaded to the same weight, the same load distribution and were flown at the same altitude and speed, with the autopilot controlling the aircraft. During these

32

The Avro Tudor was the first aircraft that I flew in as an excited five year old.

trials, officials of the Air Registration Board and the Ministry of Transport & civil aviation, Accidents investigation branch, were on board the aircraft. The asymmetric condition referred to was reproduced through causing a temporary loss of power on one side by cutting the fuel supply of the outboard engine and making a slight reduction of power to the inboard engine.

The peculiar behaviour of the automatic pilot which Captain Carreras had reported was reproduced exactly and when the autopilot was disengaged, the aircraft went into a steep spiral turn, in which considerable height was lost and a very high speed built up. It was found that as the aircraft went into this turn, the effect of the windmilling engine and the relatively low speed was to make the rudder and aileron controls virtually ineffective, until the aircraft had built up speed in the dive. During this dive, it turned in the opposite direction to it's original heading.

What the test pilots thought would happen, happened in every detail and they were of course prepared and made the necessary recovery. Captain Carreras flew with Captain Jennings when he was doing his last series of tests and he said the behaviour of the aeroplane was almost identical in every respect with that of his own aeroplane when he was flying over France.

The cause of the loss of power on one side has been analysed by the owner as being due to the incorrect use of various ancillary engine controls which are designed to guard against this sort of thing in the rather adverse conditions of icing in which the Tudor was flying at the time.

The owners freely admit that the affair was not in any way the fault of the aircraft or it's engines. The engines are the famous Rolls Royce Merlin type which are recognised as being one of the most reliable transport aircraft engines in the world. They are fitted with special safety devices to prevent them suffering loss of power when flying through the type of cloud that is likely to produce ice. Had these devices been used properly at the right time or loss of power detected before disengaging the automatic pilot, there is no doubt the incident would never have occurred.

The necessary steps to eliminate a recurrence of this nature have been taken in the form of fresh and more detailed instructions to engineers and pilots, as to how to handle their engines when these conditions are met, and how to prevent the aircraft getting in such a position when control becomes difficult in the event of unavoidable engine failures.

It is pointed out that what happened to Captain Carreras and his Tudor, could of course have happened to any type of twin-engined or four-engined aircraft under similar conditions and there can be not much doubt that it has happened many times in the past with disastrous results. It could well be the cause of fatal accidents to many aircraft which have crashed into mountains during bad weather. The owners, in order to prove this theory, carried out similar tests on three other types of aircraft, two British and one American, which they operate. The results were exactly the same as the Tudor

"The official findings and report on this Tudor incident will of course be made by the chief inspector of accidents. Aviation Traders Limited wish to make it quite clear that the statement they are publishing at this time is in no way intended to influence or hasten the official findings on this matter."

The Tudor was given a clean bill of health shortly after that demonstration flight.

Chapter 3

Dan Air and Blackbushe Airport

After living in Berlin for just over two years, our family returned to England when my Father joined the British airline Dan Air as their Chief engineer. The name Dan Air was derived from Davies and Newman, the two directors who headed a firm of shipping brokers. In 1953, Dan Air Services Ltd was registered as a subsidiary of Davies & Newman Ltd. Initially they owned a single Douglas DC-3 which they had inherited from Meredith Air Transport as collateral against money owed to Davies and Newman. At that time, the airline was based at Southend airport and operated ad hoc charters.

In 1955 the airline moved it's base to Blackbushe airport in Hampshire and established an engineering base at nearby Lasham airfield. Soon after my Father joined the company, the airline's fleet had grown to two DC-3s, four Avro Yorks, a Bristol freighter and a De Havilland Heron. They were operating inclusive tour charter flights and had begun their first scheduled service route from Blackbushe to Jersey Construction of Blackbushe airfield had first begun in 1941, and three hard runways were created in the standard military layout. The first RAF squadron took up residence in 1942.

Blackbushe was one of literally hundreds of airfields that were hastily constructed during World War Two and incredibly, Great Britain could eventually boast a total of more than six hundred airfields. An American pilot who was stationed in Britain during the war once said that the country was like a giant aircraft carrier and, when you realise how many airfields had been squeezed onto the island, you can see his point. Throughout the war, a number of fighter squadrons were based at Blackbushe and it was also a designated diversion airfield for Bomber Command.

By 1944, more than 3,000 airmen were based there. Another point of interest about Blackbushe is that FIDO had been installed at the airfield. FIDO stood for Fog Intensive Dispersal Operation and basically consisted of two pipelines that ran along the length of the runway edges. There were holes at regular intervals in the pipes and crude aviation fuel was pumped along the lines and then ignited. The heat from the burning fuel caused the fog in the immediate vicinity to disperse and improved visibility sufficiently to allow an aircraft to land. Although FIDO did actually work effectively, it was incredibly expensive in terms of fuel usage and of course, would cause today's conservationists to have an absolute fit!

In 1946, the RAF moved out and the airfield was handed over to the Ministry of Aviation, with the aim of encouraging the civilian airlines to start using it. It's location, at about 35 miles to the west of London was ideal. The A30 main road to London literally ran through the airfield (the runways were to the north of the road and the maintenance area was to the south of it.) There were nearby rail links at Blackwater and Camberley railway stations and the runways had been built with Bomber Command in mind, so were of adequate length to satisfy the needs of any civilian operators.

Another notable point in the airfield's favour, was the fact that it enjoyed a very favourable weather record. Often, when London airport was experiencing very bad visibility due to fog, the weather conditions at Blackbushe were fine. Consequently it had been nominated as the primary diversion airfield for London airport (later renamed Heathrow.)

Airlines such as Falcon, Britavia, Airwork, Silver City, Air Contractors, Eagle Airways and Dan Air based themselves at Blackbushe operating a mixture of charter flights, trooping contracts and scheduled services. Also, it later became a communications headquarters for a squadron of the United States Navy, at which time you could frequently see Lockheed Constellations and Neptunes at the airfield.

Unfortunately, in 1960, it all came to an end when the Government decided they would not renew the lease that was due on the airfield. This was a deliberate act to force some of the Blackbushe based airlines to move to the under-utilised Gatwick airport to the south of London.

Consequently, all flying at Blackbushe ceased for a while, but then Air Vice Marshall Bennett bought the airfield and it became active again in 1962.

It became home to a number of flight training organisations and then when Bennett sold the airfield to Douglas Arnold in the early 1970s, it was also home to Arnold's collection of restored Warbirds.

The airlines however, had all been forced to move elsewhere.

At the time, the country had two large State owned airlines. One was the British Overseas Airways Corporation (BOAC) and the other was British European Airways (BEA.) They were both Government owned and were given the best pickings whenever new routes or contracts were being awarded. All the other British airlines were collectively known as the 'independents' and they were left to fight for whatever was left in the way of work. This mainly comprised of ad hoc charter flights, the odd military trooping contract, or scheduled service routes to destinations that were of no interest to the two main carriers.

One of the leading 'independent' airlines was Eagle.

Chapter 4

Eagle/British Eagle International Airlines

The airline Eagle had been started by former wartime pilot Harold Bamberg, who proved to be a true pioneer in the travel industry. Following the Berlin Airlift, during which he had operated four Halifax bombers that had been converted to carry freight, he acquired a fleet of Avro Yorks.

These were kept busy, when in 1951 he was awarded a trooping contract flying between the U.K. and Singapore. The following year, Eagle moved to Blackbushe airport and built up a large fleet of Vickers Viking aircraft. With these, he started operating scheduled services.

Bamberg then bought out two travel companies, the Henry Lunn travel agency and the Polytechnic Touring Association. These were merged to form a new company called Lunn Poly. Now Eagle became the first airline to be vertically integrated with it's own travel agency and they pioneered all inclusive package holidays.

In 1957, Bamberg formed Eagle Airways (Bermuda).

Using a fleet of Vickers Viscounts, the company operated scheduled services between Bermuda and New York. The network was then extended to include Montreal, Baltimore and Washington. Eagle then acquired the first of six Douglas DC-6 aircraft for use on long haul operations.

When in 1960, Blackbushe airport was closed, Eagle transferred their operation to London Heathrow. In the same year and for the first time, more passengers crossed the Atlantic by air than by sea. Needless to say, this fact was noted with some alarm by the Cunard Steamship company. Determined to move with the times, Cunard bought a 60% shareholding in Eagle and formed a new company, Cunard Eagle Airways. This really made BOAC sit up and take notice and they were further annoyed when Bamberg pulled a clever trick. He now owned some Bristol Britannia turbo prop aircraft and promptly put them onto the Bermuda register. As Bermuda was a British colony, no reciprocal approvals were needed from the overseas authorities and Cunard Eagle could fly scheduled services across the Atlantic to Bermuda and then link up with Eagle Airways (Bermuda) schedules to America and Canada.

In 1961, Cunard Eagle was awarded a licence to operate scheduled services from London and Manchester to New York, Boston and Washington. BOAC was furious and immediately lodged an objection to the award, so the licence was revoked, pending a review.

Bamberg then put his first Boeing 707 onto the Bermuda register and started operating it between Bermuda and New York. Unknown to him, BOAC now secretly approached Cunard with a proposal to start a joint venture. To make the proposal irresistible to Cunard, BOAC offered to pay 70% of the required capital and to dedicate eight of their Boeing 707s to the operation. As BOAC was a state owned corporation, this was of course funded at the British tax payer's expense! Needless to say, Cunard probably thought that all their Christmases had come at once and the new liaison went ahead.

BOAC had viewed Bamberg's airline as a problem, so they had used their enormous state funded cash resources to make the problem go away. Bamberg was so disgusted that he bought back control of Cunard Eagle airways and formed a new company British Eagle International Airlines.

In 1963, British Eagle put Britannia aircraft on scheduled domestic routes competing directly with BEA. In the same year, they took over the airline Starways which gave them access to routes from Liverpool airport. Liverpool to Heathrow schedules then began using Vickers Viscount aircraft.

In 1964, the company won a government contract for flights between the U.K. and the Woomera rocket test range in Australia. British Eagle Engineering modified two Britannia aircraft by fitting a very large door in the forward fuselage section, which permitted the loading of the rocket parts.

When I joined British Eagle in 1965, the company was operating 17 Bristol Britannias and 7 Vickers Viscounts. They had orders in place for 3 BAC 1-11s and 2 Boeing 707-320s. Although I wasn't aware of it at the time, the company was in dispute with the Government and HMRC over a 14% tax that was payable on any imported foreign aircraft. This was a measure that had been put into place by the government to encourage British airlines to buy

British made aircraft. Eagle maintained that they should be excused from paying the levy on the grounds that there were no British made alternatives to the Boeing 707. They also pointed out that BOAC had already been granted a waiver when they purchased their Boeing 707s, thereby setting a precedent. Incredibly, these points were completely ignored by the authorities and they continued to refuse to exempt the company from the import duty. In view of this refusal, Eagle put a delay on the delivery of their Boeing 707s.

Meanwhile, the twelve newly hired engineering apprentices (including me) were blissfully unaware of these highbrow negotiations. All we knew was that we were starting work at one of Britain's leading independent airlines.

We had signed up for a four year apprenticeship during which we would gain practical experience in each of the company's various maintenance departments at Heathrow airport. This training would be interspersed with regular terms at Southall Technical college where we studied aeronautical engineering.

I vividly remember a hair-raising experience I had when working on an aircraft one day. The aircraft in question was a Bristol Britannia and it was parked inside one of the Eagle hangars undergoing a maintenance check.

When it was originally designed, the Britannia had a red rotating beacon mounted on the top of the vertical fin. The aircraft hadn't been in service for very long before it became apparent that this was a stupid location for it. Whenever a filament failed and needed to be replaced, it required specialised equipment in the form of a 'cherry-picker' to enable someone to get up to the top of the fin and change the bulb. Consequently it was decided that whenever the aircraft was due into the hangar for a maintenance check, a modification was to be carried out. This involved the fitting of a red rotating beacon unit onto the roof of the fuselage. The beauty of this modification was the fact that the filament could now be changed from inside the aircraft cabin and so cherry-pickers would no longer be needed. Part of the modification required us to disconnect and remove the old unit from the top of the aircraft's vertical fin and then fit a blanking plate in it's place. Today, it was my turn to carry out that task and I had been hoisted up on the end of the cherry picker and brought alongside the vertical fin of the aircraft. The top of the fin on the Britannia rose to a height just short of 38 feet above the ground and was actually too tall to fit inside the hangar. The aircraft would be towed in nose first, so that the wings and majority of the fuselage were under cover and just the tail section was left sticking out. The two hangar doors were then slid across towards one another and each one had a semi circular cutout which fitted the contour of the fuselage. A rubber 'skirt' attached to the cutout sections provided a reasonably snug fit to keep the wind and rain from blowing into the hangar. I had now transferred across from the cherry picker basket and was sitting astride the tail fin rather like a jockey on horseback. After the initial nervous transfer onto my high perch, I was now comfortable with the situation and engrossed in the job in front of me.

At any given moment when an aircraft is in for a major maintenance check, there are many engineers crawling all over it, simultaneously working on a multitude of jobs. One of those jobs was to remove the Proteus engines and transfer them to the power plant bay for strip down.

Vickers Viking aircraft belonging to Eagle lined up at Blackbushe airport.

Having all that weight removed from the leading edge of the wing would cause the whole wing section to twist out of shape and so to counteract this, a concrete block weighing the same as the engine would be fitted to the engine mountings. The crane that was lifting one of these blocks into position had been carefully positioning it under the guidance of some engine fitters. It was now almost in position and the crane operator was inching the block in response to the hand signals he was being given. Unfortunately, the block wasn't quite as close to the mounting brackets as they thought and when the crane released it, it thumped into place hard. This placed a sudden downward force on the leading edge of the wing, which caused the whole front portion of the aircraft to dip. Needless to say, the tail section of the aircraft rose just as suddenly in sympathy and I was catapulted upwards. For a brief moment, I remained airborne as the aircraft's tail fin dropped back down to it's original position, but then I clattered back down on top of it. I wrapped both my arms around the fin and hung on for dear life. As my colleague quickly manoeuvred the basket of the cherry picker back alongside me once again, I took a lot of persuading to release my grip! It goes without saying that today's Health & Safety assessors would have had kittens.

By the 1960s, travelling by air was becoming ever more popular and despite the huge rise in the number of flights worldwide, accidents were thankfully rare. London Heathrow is the busiest airport in Britain and during the three years that I was there with British Eagle, there were two tragic accidents that actually happened at the airport itself.

The first occurred on the 27th of October 1965. A Vickers Vanguard (G-APEE) operated by British European Airways was inbound to Heathrow where the weather was extremely poor. Fog had reduced the visibility to just 350 metres and the crew began an Instrument Landing System approach to runway 28R. Their approach was being monitored by the Precision Approach Radar controller and he noted that when the aircraft was just two miles from the runway it was drifting off the approach centreline. Just as he was about to instruct them to discontinue the approach, the pilots announced that they were going around. The visibility on runway 28L was then reported to be 500 metres and the aircraft was offered a PAR talk-down to that runway. This option had been offered because the ILS Localiser for that runway was unserviceable. G-APEE then made it's approach but it resulted in a second go around, following which they entered a holding pattern to await an improvement in the weather. Shortly afterwards, another Vanguard aircraft made a successful approach and landing onto runway 28R. No doubt encouraged by this, the crew of G-APEE announced that they intended to make another landing attempt. The pilots flew their third approach of the night, but when just seconds away from a landing, they began another go around. The First Officer initiated a rapid change to the aircraft's pitch attitude, whilst the Captain selected the flaps up. Two mistakes were then made. Instead of selecting the flaps to 20, the Captain accidentally selected them to 5. Because the First Officer had made an excessively abrupt change to the pitch attitude, the aircraft's pressure instruments momentarily gave an erroneous indication that the aircraft was climbing rapidly, when in actual fact it was still descending towards the ground. Believing that he needed to reduce the rate of climb, the First Officer pushed forward on his control column. This further increased their rate of descent and G-APEE ploughed into the ground killing all 36 people on board.

Many lessons were learned from the accident. The flight had begun late at night and ended in the early hours of the morning. Crew fatigue had almost certainly had an adverse effect on the two pilot's in terms of their performance and decision making abilities. Also, subsequent pilot training re-emphasised the fact that position error could give false pressure instrument readings, particularly during large changes in pitch attitude. A radio altimeter (which is not susceptible to position error) was subsequently installed on all the Vanguard aircraft.

One of the most significant changes following

the accident however, was the introduction of an approach ban whenever the weather conditions at an airfield dropped below an airline's approved minima. Previously, it was left to the discretion of the pilots to 'shoot an approach and take a look' if they felt it was worth doing so. Now, airlines were obliged to abide by previously approved and documented limits in terms of visibility. If the visibility was reported to be less than that limit, then they weren't even allowed to attempt an approach. This removed any temptation for reckless heroics.

Also, it was generally accepted that if an aircraft had made two unsuccessful attempts to land in bad weather, then there was little point in making a third attempt. Instead, it would be wiser to divert to an alternative airport where the weather was better. The approach ban rule remains in place to this day.

The second serious accident at Heathrow when I was based there, was on the 8th April 1968. A Boeing 707-465 operated by the British Overseas Airways Corporation (BOAC) was scheduled to fly from Heathrow to Sydney, routing via Zurich and Singapore. With 116 passengers and 11 crew aboard, the aircraft took off from runway 28L, but 20 seconds after it got airborne, the number two engine failed due to a fatigue fracture of the Low Pressure compressor. Debris from the compressor severed the fuel supply line which started a fire. When the engine failure became apparent, the captain called for the engine failure checklist to be actioned. The number two thrust lever was closed as part of this checklist and because the landing gear was already retracted, this correctly caused the gear warning horn to sound. This could be silenced by pressing a horn cancel button, but on hearing the warning, the first officer instinctively (and mistakenly) pressed the fire warning cut out. This action prevented the fire warning bell from sounding when the fuel line severed and started the fire. However, the crew did become aware of the fire because the red light illuminated on the number two fire handle (shut off switch). At this point, the captain called for the Engine fire checklist to be actioned. Unfortunately, when changing from one checklist to the other, the flight engineer missed a vital action, namely to pull the fire handle, which would shut off both the fuel and hydraulics associated with the engine. Because of this, the fire rapidly increased in intensity, to such an extent that the number two engine and part of the engine attachment pylon fell off the aircraft and into a gravel pit below.

When the aircraft declared an emergency over the radio, Air Traffic Control initially offered a return for a landing on runway 28L, but when it became apparent how serious the fire was, the crew were offered the option of landing on runway 05R as this was a shorter distance for them to fly.

Manoeuvring the aircraft to 05R was very challenging due to the reduced distance to it and the fact that there was no vertical guidance on that runway. Despite this, it was extremely well handled by the captain. Apart from the worry as to whether he could get the aircraft back onto the ground before the port wing burned through and fell off, he was also now being told by the flight engineer that his engine instruments were suggesting that they were about to lose number one engine as well. The landing gear was lowered and full flap selected, but now the hydraulic contents and pressure both started to fall. As mentioned earlier, because they had failed to operate the fire handle, this meant that the hydraulic shutoff valve hadn't been closed and this was the reason for the loss of the hydraulic contents. Fortunately, the landing gear did lock down securely, but the flaps stopped at 47 degrees, instead of the 50 degree full flap setting.

Despite everything, the captain landed the aircraft successfully and then used reverse thrust on engines 1 and 4 to help bring it to a rapid halt. Reverse thrust was maintained until the aircraft had almost come to a halt and unfortunately this deflected the flames towards the fuselage. Once they had stopped, the captain ordered the fire drill on all the remaining engines, but before this could be carried out, the fuel tanks in the port wing exploded, whereupon the captain ordered an immediate evacuation. Consequently, none of the fire handles were pulled, the fuel valves remained open and the fuel boost pumps were left on.

Despite the rapid spread of the fire, of the 127 people aboard, 112 passengers and 10 crew members evacuated the aircraft successfully, although 38 passengers were injured in the process. Tragically, 4 passengers died on board, as did one stewardess who was heroically trying to help them escape from the rear of the aircraft. The stewardess was 22 year old Barbara Jane Harrison, who was posthumously awarded the George Cross. This is the highest award for bravery that can be bestowed upon a civilian by the British government.

The evacuation was practically complete by the time the emergency services arrived at the scene and the aircraft was totally destroyed by fire. It had come to rest very close to the British Eagle hangars and was a truly horrific sight.

Once again, as is always the case, many lessons

were learned in the subsequent accident enquiry. The airport fire service had been criticised for poor deployment of appliances and equipment failures. Following this, changes were made to their procedures and the fire fighting equipment was modified and improved. It was also recognised that the BOAC emergency checklists and the manner in which they were to be actioned needed to be revised.

A new 'engine fire or severe failure' checklist was created, which now combined the two previous engine failure and engine fire checklists. This meant that there was now no chance of missing out a vital item, unlike before, when switching from one drill to another.

Although the aircraft wreckage was soon removed, it stood outside our hangars for a while as a stark reminder of the disastrous consequences when things go wrong in our industry.[1]

On Wednesday 6th November 1968, I was sitting in a classroom at Heathrow airport learning about the electrical systems on the Boeing 707. Our lesson was suddenly interrupted and we were informed that an emergency meeting was to be held at the Eagle hangars. Shortly after joining the assembled crowd outside the hangars, we were informed that the airline had gone bust. Along with two thousand of my colleagues, I had just lost my job.At the time, the airline had been operating twenty four aircraft. Three Boeing 707s, five BAC 1-11s, twelve Bristol Britannias and four Vickers Viscounts.

Fortunately for me, some days later I was informed that the Civil Air Transport Industry Training Board

1   Runway 05/23 was normally only used when wind speed and direction prevented the use of the main Runways 10/28. It was completely withdrawn from use in 2002.

had agreed to take on the British Eagle apprentices in order to complete our training. They subsequently arranged for us to attend RAF Halton in Bedfordshire. This, of course, was the very same place where my Father had trained more than thirty years before. The facilities at Halton were excellent and shortly after I completed my training there, I was offered a job with the British Overseas Airways Corporation (BOAC.) I began work as an electrician on BOAC's fleet of Boeing 707 aircraft at London Heathrow airport.

The burning aircraft shortly after landing on runway 05R.

Number two engine (circled) can be seen falling from G-ARWE. Fuel is streaming from the damaged left wing. The engine fell into a gravel pit so nobody on the ground was injured.

Chapter 5

British Overseas Airways Corporation (BOAC)

I initially worked in Technical block B, a very large hangar built on BOAC's maintenance area at London Heathrow airport. This was where the 'heavy' maintenance work was carried out and aircraft were rotated through the facility on a regular and pre planned basis. One side of the huge building was dedicated to the Vickers VC-10 fleet and the other side to the Boeing 707 fleet. I was assigned to the Boeing 707s and, following an in-house course, given company approval to sign off maintenance work on the type.

Occasionally an aircraft was brought in for unscheduled work, which usually happened following an incident of some kind. On one memorable occasion, one of the company's B.707s had suffered an in-flight engine fire in its number one (left outboard) engine. The engine fire extinguishers had eventually put out the blaze, but not before a significant amount of damage had been done to the engine, it's pylon and the wing section surrounding it. Shortly after the aircraft landed and the passengers had disembarked, the aircraft was towed across to our hangar and brought inside. It was a mess.

After detailed inspections had been carried out and discussions had taken place between the airline and aircraft manufacturer, a specialist team of engineers from Boeing arrived on site and began their own investigations. They concluded that the whole of the outer wing section had to be removed and a replacement section 'stitched' on in it's place. This was ground breaking work and was fascinating to witness. The airframe fitters installed the new wing section and then my colleagues and I spliced in new looms of electrical cables to replace the original charred and ruined wiring. It was a huge job, but with the supervision and guidance provided by the Boeing team, it was completed with surprising speed. A real 'one off' repair job and once complete, the aircraft was returned to service. A rare and satisfying break from the routine maintenance cycles.

During the time I was working for BOAC at London Heathrow, I remember a couple of amusing incidents that happened.

The Boeing 707 has an area forward of the front cargo hold. It is called 'Lower 41' and can be accessed via a hatch in the floor of the flight deck. This area is actually the electronics bay and houses a complex array of electrical cables, bus bars & circuit breakers. Needless to say, as an electrician I found myself down in the electronics bay on many occasions. It was extremely cramped down there and you were forced to crawl around on your stomach, trying not to graze various body parts on some of the sharp objects and panels along the way. One day, one of our engineering supervisors was down there along with a newly hired engineer. He was showing the new guy the location of various electrical components, terminal blocks and bus bars. Prior to climbing in there, he had grabbed a large torch and he was now waving it around to direct it's beam onto whatever component he was talking about at the time. The torch was a very sturdy metal framed item and whilst waving it around, he brushed it against a live bus bar. This resulted in a blinding flash, a shower of sparks and a series of loud expletives. Temporarily blinded by the flash, it took him a few moments to regain his sight, whereupon he saw that the shower of sparks had set fire to one of the insulating blankets that lined the inside of the fuselage alongside him. In a matter of seconds, the flames spread to the adjoining blankets setting them alight too. Various people rapidly evacuated the area including our supervisor. He then quickly grabbed a fire extinguisher, ducked back into the electronics bay and put the fire out. Fortunately there was very little damage and everything was put right in no time at all. The flame resistant insulation blankets hadn't proved to be very flame resistant at all, but this was deemed to be because they had become contaminated with dirt and grease over time. They were immediately replaced with new ones. What was amusing is that the supervisor was commended by the airline management for his bravery in extinguishing the fire, thereby preventing serious damage to the aircraft. What seems to have been overlooked is the fact that he had started the fire in the first place!

Another incident that took place happened when I was working in the flight deck of a Boeing 707. The aircraft was in the hangar undergoing a major maintenance check. As always, engineers were working side by side in numerous locations on the aircraft. I was seated in one of the pilot's seats and was busy replacing some wiring behind the forward instrument panel. One of my colleagues was working nearby on an electrical panel. Suddenly I heard him curse and the screwdriver he had been holding clattered down behind the panel. This seemed to coincide with a loud whooshing noise from outside the aircraft, followed by some loud shouts of alarm.

'What was that?' This came from my colleague who now had a worried expression on his face. I stuck my head out of the open side window and looked back at the left wing and engines. A strange 'mist' appeared to be drifting away from the number two engine, whilst an engineer who had been working on the engine was picking himself up from the floor. It was apparent that my colleague (or rather his screwdriver) had somehow triggered the fire extinguisher for the number two engine. The engineer who had been working on it at the time, had now picked himself off the floor and was heading our way at a gallop.

I said, 'It looks like you've blown the fire extinguisher and someone isn't very happy about it.' The engineer burst into the flight deck, quickly took in the scene and realised what must have happened. He was an Irishman who was always quietly spoken and generally kept himself to himself. Without a word, he grabbed my colleague by the throat and pinned him up against the wall of the flight deck. Clenching the fist of his free hand, he prepared to deliver a punch but then thought better of it. Releasing my terrified colleague, he said, 'You frightened the bejesus out of me you bloody idiot.' With that, he turned on his heel and went back outside. The two of them shook hands and made their peace a short while later.

Chapter 6

The Boeing 747

You would have thought that the BOAC pilots who were earmarked to fly the brand new Boeing 747 would have been tripping over one another trying to get to the front of the queue. However, that isn't what happened at all. Instead, they decided to go on strike. They were holding out for more money and had submitted a proposed 'wide body salary' (the wide body referring of course to the twin aisle Boeing 747).

Their argument was that the new aircraft carried far more passengers than other types and this heaped increased responsibility onto the shoulders of the pilots who were to fly them. This was a rather insulting and deeply flawed argument, because it suggested that a B.707 pilot was pretty relaxed about flying 150 passengers around, but if expected to fly a B.747 with 365 passengers aboard, they were actually going to have to start taking the job seriously. It was a ridiculous premise and if you were to ask an airline pilot if it makes any difference if there are 10 or 1,000 people sitting behind them, then they would say that they always strive to get the aircraft back down in one piece. After all, if they are sitting at the very front of the aircraft, they will be the first ones to arrive at the scene of the crash if they get it wrong.

Irrespective of the motive behind the threatened strike action, the pilots were determined to win a substantial pay rise in return for flying the Boeing 747. The airline's management were equally determined to refuse to give in to their demands. Unfortunately, the strike went ahead and the sad sight of a line of shiny new Boeing 747s could be seen parked outside the BOAC maintenance hangars. In the meantime, amidst much flag waving publicity, Pan Am and TWA were now flying in and out of London Heathrow in their brand new Boeing 747s.

It is sometimes said that the downside to being the first to operate a new aircraft type is that your airline will have to endure the inevitable teething problems that will occur in the early days of operation. No matter how much planning and preparation an airline carries out before introducing a new aircraft type into service, nobody knows exactly what problems are going to arise. Defects will inevitably occur and of course the engineers won't have encountered them before. Over time, they will know exactly what caused those defects and the best way to fix them. Over time, those components or systems will have been modified or redesigned so that they no longer fail or cause problems. Overall reliability will be improved, aircraft downtime reduced, utilisation increased and everyone will be happy. Other airlines that subsequently start operating that aircraft type now have the benefit of those modified and improved systems. Their engineers have the benefit of bulletins and maintenance directives that highlight any past difficulties and provide guidance as to how they can be overcome. Sometimes, not being the first does have it's advantages.

This was definitely the case with the Boeing 747. The Boeing 747-100 was a truly remarkable aircraft and represented an enormous leap forward in aviation. With its hugely increased passenger capacity, it reduced the seat mile cost for an airline by over 30%. This resulted in significantly reduced airfares and offered long distance air travel to a much wider audience. Boeing gambled the company on the 747, and the gamble paid off. With a number of different variants appearing over the years, the aircraft went on to enjoy an incredible 54 year production run with well over 1,500 aircraft being sold. However, the early 100 series model had a big flaw: the engines.

The engines of course were not made by Boeing, but by the long established and respected American manufacturer Pratt & Whitney. Their engines even had a decal on the side of the cowling that sported the proud slogan 'Pratt & Whitney, Dependable Engines.' The engine manufacturer had been working with Boeing from day one of the 747's conception, to design and produce the huge high bypass turbo fan engine that would power the beast. The result was the JT9D-3A, an engine that produced 43,500 lbs of thrust. Amazing though it was, it proved to be very problematic. It was susceptible to compressor stalls, an occurrence that would send the exhaust gas temperature off the clock and wreck the engine in the space of seconds. In flight, it was found that the fan casing was warping, a condition that became known as Ovalizing. As the casing became misshapen, the fine gap between it and the rotating fan blades reduced to the point where the blades started to rub and dig into it. At best this resulted in a loss of thrust. In the worst case it resulted in complete blade failure and fracture. Another problem was associated with a surge bleed valve. When thrust was reduced in order to begin a descent, the bleed valve problem resulted in a severe over temperature condition, which necessitated a Boroscope inspection after landing. More often than not, this showed that the engine had been seriously damaged and needed to be removed and replaced.

Pan Am and TWA thought that their engine spares holding was sufficient to last them for ages but in no time at all, they had used them all. In fact, they used all the JT9D engines that Pratt and Whitney had produced so far.

Knowing that BOAC were not flying any of their 747s because of the industrial dispute, they came to an arrangement whereby they would take all BOAC's spare engines and even some of the engines that were fitted to their immobile aircraft. Needless to say, BOAC made sure that it was a very lucrative arrangement as far as they were concerned. Now the sad line up of BOAC 747s at Heathrow looked even sadder because the aircraft's engines had been replaced by concrete blocks that hung on the wing pylons in their place.

The alarming number of engine changes started to reduce, following the introduction of a number of engine handling 'tweaks and tricks' that the pilots and flight engineers were employing when operating the aircraft. Increasing or decreasing thrust on the engines was done very slowly and carefully whenever possible. The use of reverse thrust after landing was avoided if there was a significant cross wind blowing across the runway to avoid the likelihood of compressor stalls. The engines were also being operated at a reduced thrust setting for takeoff and climb, but this of course, had a serious impact on the aircraft's performance. The takeoff weight had to be significantly reduced, meaning it could carry fewer passengers and/or less fuel for each flight. Needless to say, there was a veritable army of people working on a solution to the problems. One of the most significant redesign solutions came in the form of a new engine mounting arrangement. A completely new thrust frame yoke was designed. This yoke affair now mounted the engine to the wing pylon and provided sufficient rigidity to prevent the dreaded Ovalizing of the fan casing. That design, plus other modifications completely resolved the early issues with the engine. The Pratt & Whitney JT9D was now a dependable engine. What is more, other engine options later became available with power plants being offered by General Electric (the GE CF6) and Rolls Royce (the RB 211.)

Meanwhile, BOAC's industrial dispute continued to rumble on. The engineering division took full advantage of this, by putting the aircraft into the hangar for some modification work to be carried out. This was originally to be done over an extended period so that it didn't disrupt the flying programme. Currently there was no flying programme, so the work could be completed in one hit. As soon as one aircraft had been done, the next one was wheeled into the hangar.

So it was, that I found myself working on the 747 more often than I worked on the 707.

Chapter 7

Flying Lessons at Blackbushe

When my Dad joined Dan Air as their Chief Engineer, the company's chief Inspector was a man called Frank Horridge. They became good friends and shared a love of flying small aircraft. Frank had started a company based at Lasham airfield called Air Tows. They operated a number of single engined aircraft that towed gliders up to a pre arranged altitude. Then, once the glider had released itself from the tow line, the tug aircraft would quickly land and get hitched up to the next waiting glider. As Lasham was the busiest gliding site in the U.K, Frank's aircraft were kept hard at work. He then added another string to his bow by becoming a director and part owner of a flying school at Blackbushe airport. It was called Three Counties Aero Club and I had worked there as a holiday job during the summer when I was a schoolboy. I spent the days working in the hangars at the western end of the airfield with an engineer by the name of Pete Townsend.

We spent some time repairing the damaged wing of an Auster aircraft. After repairing the damaged structure of the wing, we covered sections of it with new fabric and then applied dope to the fabric using a paint brush. I remember becoming quite light headed with the fumes from the dope and found the smell very pleasant. Probably an indication that I should avoid glue sniffing as I would quickly end up an addict? Anyway, I really enjoyed my holiday job at the Three Counties Aero Club even when I wasn't getting high on aviation dope.

Now years later, I made a decision: I didn't want to fix aircraft. Instead, I wanted to fly them. Naturally, if I was going to take flying lessons in order to get a private pilot's licence (PPL), then it made sense that I did it at Three counties aero club. I was just about to celebrate my 21st birthday at the time and my parents said that in order to get me started, they would pay for some flying lessons as a birthday present. I couldn't have asked for a better present.

Over the next few weeks I was kept busy with my job at Heathrow and we also had a spell of miserable weather throughout January. Consequently, it wasn't until February 1970 that I started my first flying lesson. Looking at my pilot's log book, I can see the first entry: "3rd February 1970. G-AXBE (a Beagle Pup). Instructor Derek Johnson. Local flight from Blackbushe. One hour duration. Exercises 1 to 5."

Later that same day, Derek and I again took to the air in a different Beagle Pup (G-AWWF) The following day, we went up in G-AXBE again and spent an hour covering exercises 6 to 8. I was totally hooked. I loved every second of it and didn't want it to end.

My first three flying lessons had been in the Beagle Pup. The Pup was a good aircraft with nicely harmonised controls, a comfortable cockpit with side by side seating and tricycle undercarriage to make life easier for ground handling. However, I had been looking at the aero club's price list and had noted the hourly rates for hiring the various aircraft in their fleet. Whilst the Pup wasn't the most expensive, it wasn't the cheapest either and I noted that honour was held by the Piper Cub. With cost driving my initial curiosity, I was further intrigued by the aircraft itself. It was an early Piper J3 Cub built in the 1940s. Unlike the aluminium clad Beagle Pup, the Cub had fabric covering it's wings, fuselage and tail plane. It had a tail wheel configuration, with tandem seating instead of the side by side layout in the Pup. The cylinder heads of the small 65 horsepower engine were exposed to the airflow (for better cooling) so they stuck out on either side of the engine cowling. To start the Beagle Pup, you turned a key on the instrument panel and a starter motor spun the engine into life. To start the Piper Cub, you grabbed hold of one of the wooden propellor blades and then swung your arm down in an arc to pull the blade smartly around. With luck, there followed a cough and splutter and the engine wheezed into life. I made my mind up there and then. This was the aircraft for me. From that day onwards, all my flying lessons were to be in the old J3 Cub.

When flying the J-3 Cub, the student pilot sat in the rear cockpit, with the instructor seated in front of them. This was because when it came to flying solo, this had to be done from the rear cockpit and so it was better to get a student used to flying from that position to begin with.

Interestingly, this was not the case with the Piper super Cub which was flown from the front cockpit when solo. Although the aero club did buy some super Cubs later, at the time that I was undergoing training they only had the one J-3 Cub. Needless to say, with an instructor sitting directly in front of you, your view ahead was severely restricted and you spent all your time tilting your head to the left and right in order to peer over the instructor's left and right shoulder. There were no instruments in the rear cockpit, so once again you were forced to crane your head from side to side in order to see the instruments on the forward panel. Not that there were many of them. There was an engine Rev counter, an altimeter, an airspeed indicator, a compass, an oil temperature gauge and an oil pressure gauge. That was it, apart from a slip indicator in the form of a bubble in a glass tube. The fuel tank was located ahead of the front pilot and had been positioned (rather disconcertingly) directly above their legs. The filler cap was outside the cockpit just ahead of the windscreen and the method of displaying the fuel contents was beautifully simple. There was a hole drilled in the filler cap and a thin metal Rod protruded up through it.

Attached to the bottom end of the Rod was a cork that floated on the fuel in the tank. You could instantly see how much fuel was in the tank by how much of the Rod was sticking up above the filler cap. It wasn't marked with any kind of graduations, you just kept an eye on it as it got progressively shorter during the flight. When there was only a couple of inches still protruding, it was time to find somewhere to land and refuel.

It was designed using the KISS principle (Keep It Simple Stupid.) Like all aircraft with a tail wheel configuration, the forward view when on the ground in a Cub is not good. This is particularly true for the person in the rear cockpit when someone is seated in front of them. It is therefore necessary to weave the aircraft from side to side when taxiing so that you can ensure the way ahead is clear. To get in and out of the aircraft, the side window on the starboard side of the aircraft is hinged at the top. You can then swing it up and clip it flat against the underside of the wing. The small door below the window is hinged at the bottom so this can be folded down against the lower fuselage. When taxiing on the ground, it is best to leave the window and door open so you can lean out and see what is up ahead. Also, in warm weather, it is great to fly along in the cruise with them open, so that you can enjoy a cooling breeze and a fabulous view.

Anybody who has flown a tail wheel aircraft will confirm that they are a good deal trickier to handle on the ground than tricycle gear types. Both takeoff and landing require your full attention and some nifty footwork at times, particularly when landing in a crosswind. My instructor Derek Johnson used to joke that the landing wasn't over until you had climbed out of the aircraft and returned to the clubhouse. What he meant by that, of course, was that pilots have been known to make an excellent approach and touchdown on the runway, but then allow their concentration to wane just a little as the aircraft begins to slow down. Next thing they know, the tail has started to swing and before they can catch it, there is a screeching of tortured tyres, they have performed a ground loop and find themselves facing the way they have just come. I'm delighted to say, that thanks to Derek's timely prompts and warnings after I had landed, I never did suffer the harsh embarrassment of the dreaded ground loop.

The Piper Cub is many things, but nobody has ever called it fast. If you are planning on making a cross country trip in a Cub, then you will need two things. A bit of fuel and a lot of patience. If you found yourself flying along parallel to a nice straight road, after a while you couldn't help noticing that some of the cars on that road were travelling as fast as you were. If you were flying into a headwind, then embarrassingly, most of the cars were travelling faster than you were.

Consequently, a planned cross country trip needed all the usual calculations of tracks, wind velocity, drift angle, headings, distances, groundspeed, elapsed time and finally, a visit to the toilet. Even short distances took a long time so you definitely needed to have a 'nervous pee' before setting off.

On one particular cross country navigation exercise, I enjoyed an amusing incident. I was flying with an instructor whom I had only flown with once before. He was a rather serious guy who didn't smile much and had a reputation for being rather hard work to get on with at times. His other claim to fame was that he had a prosthetic leg. Quite how much of his leg was artificial I didn't know (it's not something that generally comes up in casual conversation) but needless to say, he had managed to satisfy the aviation medical authorities that he was perfectly capable of flying an aircraft despite his handicap. Being fully familiar with stories of Douglas Bader who had lost both his legs in a flying accident, but later went on to fly in the Battle of Britain, I knew that such physical difficulties could be overcome, but nonetheless, it was still rather novel to find yourself flying with a one legged instructor.

To climb in and out of a Piper Cub, a person has to be reasonably agile. Whilst there is no requirement to be athletic, a degree of agility is most definitely needed. With the floor of the cockpit set reasonably high and the undeniably awkward location of the wing strut, clambering in is a bit of an art form. The rear cockpit seat is the easier of the two to get into. As for the front seat, that is a rather more challenging task. Whichever seat you are planning to climb into, suffice to say, female pilots are definitely advised to avoid wearing skirts. With practice, a pilot can place one hand on the wing strut, the other on the seat back and, with a bold flowing action, sweep their feet above the bottom of the door sill, continue around in a graceful arc and then drop their legs neatly into the footwell whilst simultaneously plonking their bottom onto the seat.

My 'one legged instructor' had told me to climb into the rear cockpit, which I did. He then went to the front of the aircraft in order to swing the prop. Between the two of us, we then carried out the start sequence and got the engine going. I was then impressed to see my instructor swing effortlessly into the seat in front of me. He'd clearly done that before.

We were about to fly from Blackbushe to Oxford Kidlington as part of my cross country navigation training. The Piper wasn't fitted with a radio, so we had telephoned Oxford ATC for prior permission to make the flight. Now as we were taxiing out at Blackbushe, we did our engine runs and magneto checks at the runway holding point and then looked across at the control tower for clearance to line up on the runway and takeoff. The clearance was given in the form of a green signalling light that the tower controller flashed at us. We duly lined up, took off and then set course for Oxford.

My log book shows that from 'off chocks' at Blackbushe to 'on chocks' at Oxford took us 45 minutes. We then refuelled the aircraft, because we were planning to fly to Portsmouth for the second leg of my navigation exercise. The refueller was a very personable guy who chatted away merrily whilst he topped up our tank. Once the process was complete, my instructor went around to the front of the aircraft in order to swing the prop for start up. The refueller told him 'if you want to jump in, I can swing the prop for you.' This was unusual, because people generally didn't offer to do this job as they were understandably wary of getting anywhere near propellors. My instructor was delighted to accept the guy's kind offer and made a move to climb aboard. As usual, he positioned his body and hands in the required positions in preparation to making his Tarzan-like swing into the cockpit. Sadly, something about his timing clearly went wrong, because as his legs swung in towards the cockpit, there was a loud 'clang.'

He slumped into his seat at approximately the same time that I spotted his artificial leg fall to the ground just outside the aircraft. There was a moment of silence, during which the stunned look on the refueller's face was an absolute picture as he stared in total disbelief at the leg that was lying on the grass. The silence was then broken by my instructor shouting 'don't just stare at the bloody thing. Give it here.' The refueller gingerly picked up the prosthetic leg and handed it over. My instructor fastened it back into place and then said 'come on then. Let's get on with it!' I'm pretty sure that poor fuel guy at Oxford will never forget our visit there. He might still be standing there now with his mouth wide open in shock?

Once I got my private pilot's licence, I was keen to build on my flying experience by jumping into an aircraft as often as possible. Unfortunately, every time I did climb into an aircraft, it took another chunk out of my bank account. The flying instructors at Three Counties Aero Club knew only too well that I was keen to fly but could rarely afford it, so they put some free flying my way now and then. Occasionally one of the club's aircraft had been taken to Lasham airfield for maintenance. One of the instructors would phone me and ask if I was available to fly the aircraft from Lasham to Blackbushe. They would then take me by car to Lasham and drop me off there to fly the aircraft back. It was a very short distance between the two airfields, but they wouldn't complain when it took a surprisingly long time for me to complete the journey. They knew I had taken full advantage of my 'free' flight and just so long as I didn't take too long, they said nothing.

On another occasion, an instructor by the name of Mike John phoned me to ask if I fancied a bit of free flying. A student pilot he had been teaching, worked for the Automobile Association as a restaurant critic. He had the job of visiting restaurants, sampling their food and service, then writing a report and awarding a 'star' score based on his findings.

He had done this on a National basis, but now he had the idea of checking out the feasibility of hopping across the English Channel in a light aircraft to nearby continental airports such as Le Touquet, Ostend and Paris. Better still as far as I was concerned, he wasn't bothered about flying the aircraft himself, but instead just wanted to sit in the back. He had explained that it would enable him to sample the wine as well as the food in the airport restaurant. I never did find out if this was a pet project of his, or an idea his employer had come up with. Because he had an

interest in aviation, I assumed it was his idea, but I didn't care either way just so long as the Automobile

A Piper J-3 Cub similar to the one in which I learned to fly.

Association was picking up the tab.

I was extremely grateful to Mike John for calling me up, because he said I could do all the flying and he would be my instructor / co-pilot. We had a great day out. The aircraft was a Piper Arrow 180R, and was the first aircraft I had flown with retractable gear. We flew from Blackbushe to Gatwick (where we cleared customs) and then to Toussus Le Noble on the outskirts of Paris. After our 'restaurant appraisal' during which we enjoyed a fine meal, we flew back to Blackbushe via Gatwick once again. It really was a great day out.

Sadly Mike died in an aircraft he was piloting a few years later. The post mortem suggested that he suffered a heart attack shortly after taking off. He was the sole occupant.

Chapter 8

Aerobatics

My love of aerobatics had initially been sparked by Derek Johnson, who hadn't needed to be asked twice when I suggested he might demonstrate some aerobatic manoeuvres at the end of one of our flying lessons together.

I now booked myself some aerobatic lessons with him (Exercise 21 in official parlance) and we flew a number of times together in Beagle Pups and a Tiger Moth. I absolutely loved the feeling of freedom and control when swooping and soaring through a series of loops, rolls and stall turns.

Flying aerobatics calls for greater feel and co-ordination on the controls than more sedate and conventional manoeuvres, and when you hit the sweet spot and get it just right, it is immensely satisfying. Mind you, get it wrong and it is stomach churning and embarrassing in equal measure.

On one occasion, I took a friend and work colleague up to do some Aeros. Pete Finnigan had been an apprentice with me at British Eagle and now we both worked on the same shift team at BOAC. He lived near Blackbushe airport and I had taken him up in the Piper Cub on a previous trip. On this particular day, we went up in the Beagle Pup 150, with the intention of doing some aeros. I had brought along a movie camera and Pete was going to film it all. It started out well and we had completed a number of manoeuvres very nicely, but then I pulled the aircraft's nose up with the intention of doing a roll off the top. When we were inverted at the top of the manoeuvre, the speed was lower than it should be so when I applied aileron to start the half roll, the aircraft proved reluctant to respond. I thought I'd help things along with a bit of rudder. Wrong!

We fell inverted and out of control for a few seconds and then, having got the nose of the aircraft slightly below the horizon, we gained enough speed for the aircraft to respond to the roll demand. Having got the aircraft the right way up, Pete, who had stoically kept his finger on the trigger of the movie camera throughout all this, said 'Hey, I can see the propellor all of a sudden!' He was right of course and the reason that he could see the prop was because when we had been inverted, we had experienced negative G for long enough to starve the engine of fuel. Consequently, it had decided to stop running.

The prop had stopped in the vertical 12 o' clock/6 o' clock position and so was now nicely in frame for our suddenly very interesting movie. To cut a long story short, there followed a period during which I attempted to restart the engine, but without any response. Following some pumping on the fuel primer whilst I simultaneously began searching for a suitable field for a dead stick landing, the engine finally burst into life.

Now that the drama was over, Pete calmly said

'The air accident investigators aren't going to need to study our movie after all.'

I then set us up for another roll off the top (Immelmann) manoeuvre. I was working on the age old principle that if you get thrown off your horse, you should immediately remount and try again. This time I got it right. Incidentally, Pete later went on to become a Flight Engineer on the Boeing 707 with BOAC.

Another way for the holder of a private pilot's licence to clock up some flying hours was to get work flying a glider tug aircraft. You weren't paid for your efforts, so it didn't break the 'not for hire or reward' rule, but it enabled the pilot to build up their flying hours without having to pay for it. I enquired at Lasham airfield and discovered that they were always on the lookout for more glider Tug pilots. However, they did insist quite reasonably, that their tug pilots knew what was going on at both ends of the tow line, so they wanted them to have some gliding experience.

I bought myself some lessons with an instructor flying gliders.The gliding fraternity are usually a really nice bunch of people and that was certainly the case at Lasham. They are all at the airfield for the same reason. Namely to have a good time. On days when there was little thermal activity, the flights may have been short, but the good humour was always still evident. I admired the way everyone mucked in, pushing gliders into position, sorting out the tow lines, refuelling the tug aircraft, keeping a tab on who was next to fly. In fact doing whatever was necessary to keep the show on the road. Infectious enthusiasm. And then there is the flying, of course. There's no engine, he gentle sound of the whistling wind and the bird-like soaring. Brilliant!

It is probably the purest form of flight and it certainly put a smile on my face.

Chapter 9

Training For My Commercial Pilot's Licence

On a cold winter's day, I arrived at Air Service Training, the flight school at Scone airfield near Perth in Scotland. I had a very intensive course ahead of me, which was going to need a lot of hard work and study both in the classroom and in the air.

After I had been there for a while, I fell out with the flying instructor who I'd been teamed up with. A real personality clash had developed between us and something had to be done about it. I requested a change of instructor and one of the people that I subsequently flew with was a lovely guy called Danny Thompson. We got on really well and with his excellent instruction, I was quickly back on track. Danny had previously been in the RAF with treble one squadron, flying the Hawker Hunter. They became known as the Black Arrows, an aerobatic team that was one of the forerunners to the Red Arrows RAF display team. In 1958, the Black Arrows set a world record that stands to this day. At the prestigious SBAC Airshow at Farnborough, they performed a loop with 22 Hunters flying in close formation. Once I discovered

Danny was an aerobatics aficionado, whenever we flew one of the school's Cessna Aerobats, I nagged him to round off our flying lesson with a few minutes of aerobatics. He didn't need much persuading.

Whilst on the subject of aerobatics, we had some celebrity visitors during the Summer of 1973 in the form of the Rothmans aerobatic team. This was a team that flew their Pitt's Specials at Airshows and public events all around Europe. I had first seen them in action in 1970 at the annual Blackbushe airshow, at which time they were flying Stampe biplanes. Now they were flying the more modern and incredibly agile Pitts Special biplanes. They were booked to do a number of aerobatic displays at various locations around Scotland and at the end of each day would be basing themselves at our airfield.

The legendary Neil Williams was temporarily leading the team and was a man who I had hero worshipped for years. Many times winner of the British Aerobatic Championship, European aerobatic champion, a graduate of the Empire Test Pilot's School, Spitfire display pilot, film pilot and pilot of many of the vintage flying machines from the Shuttleworth collection. The list of the man's achievements was seemingly endless. Even though I was in awe of the man, I did manage to strike up a conversation and hung onto his every word whilst trying not to act like some kind of star struck groupie.

The day the team left, they put on a 'thank you for having us' display overhead Scone airfield which was a real treat for everyone. Then, Neil Williams, who was going to be competing in the European aerobatic championship later that year put on a solo display that was absolutely jaw dropping. I watched his display sequence from the balcony of the control tower and after it was over he went to the top of my 'Legendary pilots' chart.

When I first arrived at Perth, one of the Nigerian students was ready to do his qualifying cross country flight. He was tasked with flying from Scone to Aberdeen. After landing and refuelling at Aberdeen, he was then to fly onwards to Inverness. His first attempt had to be abandoned shortly after he took off from Scone. An instructor who had left Aberdeen and was heading for Scone radioed to report that the visibility in the Aberdeen area had deteriorated suddenly, so our Nigerian friend was told to turn around and return. A couple of days later, he tried again, but was again told to abandon his attempt and return. A few days later, our frustrated pilot once again set off for his third attempt at the cross country flight.

Midway between Scone and Aberdeen, a southbound aircraft reported conditions of thick fog and rain in his area. They instructed our man to turn around and head back to Scone. They were alarmed to hear the guy radio back that he had no intention of returning. He said he was fed up with all the cancelled flights and he was going to press on and do the flight this time. Despite repeated radio calls instructing him to return, they received no further response from him.

Everyone anxiously waited in the operations room at Scone for further news. Air traffic controllers at Aberdeen were advised of the situation and they promised to get in contact if they had any news. Everyone began to fear the worst. Based on the aircraft's last position report and assuming it had continued towards Aberdeen, it was now well past his estimated time of arrival and nobody had heard from him.

When flying the Cessna 150, we used to carry a small flip chart booklet that contained all our checklists. There were preflight checks, engine start checks, before takeoff checks, etc. Following those normal checks, it then outlined some emergency drills for engine failure, electrical failure, fire and smoke drills, etc. Finally, on the back cover of the booklet, there was a checklist outlining what to do following a forced landing. From memory, I recall that this covered items such as ensuring that the fuel and electrics were all switched off in the cockpit, then getting yourself well clear of the aircraft if it had been damaged and you suspected there was risk of fire. Assuming you were in an isolated area, you were then to secure the aircraft and set off to look for help. You were instructed to make your way to the nearest telephone (no mobile phones in those days) and once you found one, you were to call the number shown on the page. If you had no money you could ask the operator to make it a reverse charge call and this would be put through. The phone number that was quoted was a direct line to the flight operations office at Scone.

After an interminable wait for news of the missing flight, the operations phone rang. The duty instructor answered the phone after the very first ring. His side of the ensuing conversation went something like this: 'Hello, Scone airfield operations here. Duty instructor speaking... Oh thank God it's you, we've been worried sick... Are you okay? What happened? Where are you calling from? What do you mean you don't know where you are? You are in someone's house... Okay... Now what exactly has happened?' 'You've Crashed! Are you sure you are alright? Well thank goodness you are okay. Is the aircraft damaged at all? It is... Okay. Is it still flyable? You don't think so... Why don't you think it's still flyable? What do you mean it's got no wings?'

The aircraft arrived back at the airfield the next day on the back of a truck. Our intrepid pilot was quite right. It didn't have any wings attached to it. They had been laid in the back of the truck alongside the mangled and barely recognisable fuselage. Another compressed and twisted lump of metal lay in a corner of the truck. That turned out to be the engine. Other assorted bits and pieces littered the floor of the truck and completed the scene of destruction.

Nobody could work out how the hell the pilot had survived and climbed from the wreckage with barely a scratch on him. His explanation as to what had happened was like something out of a far fetched action movie.

He admitted that he had received the radio call to return to Scone, but felt that the weather didn't look too bad where he was, so he had decided to press on. A short while later, the weather did deteriorate quite significantly and he kept having to reduce altitude in order to maintain visual contact with the ground and to stay below the lowering cloud base. He then became unsure of his position and shortly afterwards, realised he was flying down a valley with higher ground on either side of him. He couldn't see the top of the valley sides because they were immersed in cloud.

Only now did he decide that perhaps he should turn back towards Scone, but unfortunately he had become disoriented and wasn't sure what heading he needed to fly in order to get there. The aircraft was fitted with a single ADF receiver (Automatic Direction Finding receiver) and although he hadn't received any training on the use of ADF, he believed that the needle on the relative bearing indicator always pointed at Scone. Of course this was wrong on so many levels! He said that he became confused to see the needle on the relative bearing indicator slowly sweeping around the dial in a totally erratic fashion. Of course, this was hardly surprising because he was flying too low and too far away to be able to pick up the Perth NDB (Non Directional Beacon). Asked if he knew the frequency and ident of the NDB, he admitted that he didn't, but stated that he thought the ADF receivers in the Scone aircraft were always tuned to that beacon.

Because the needle on the instrument was moving erratically and wasn't making any sense, he wondered if the ADF needed 'turning on or turning up or something?' He admitted that he may have become somewhat preoccupied as he fiddled with the ADF radio for a while, because when he looked up and stared out of the window, it was now filled with the sight of the valley wall rushing towards him. He instinctively pulled back hard on the control yoke and this action almost certainly saved his life. The aircraft pitched up violently, causing the forward speed to rapidly decay, and then the lower part of the fuselage slammed into the valley wall.

Both wings were sheared off in the impact. The engine, having been struck hard from below, was snapped off it's mountings and partly crushed. The fuselage had also been significantly distorted, making it impossible for the pilot to open his door when he attempted to leave the aircraft. He then noticed that the windscreen was no longer in place, so he managed to escape the aircraft by crawling through the empty window frame. After a few moments collecting his thoughts, he glanced around the mist shrouded hillside that was now littered with what was left of his aircraft. At this stage it probably dawned on him that his cross country flying might be over for the day.

Following the instructions in his checklist booklet, he set off down the hill in search of help. After a while, through the rolling mist and fog, he spotted a small cottage and made his way towards it. He knocked on the door and asked the startled person who answered, if he could use their telephone.

I would have paid good money to see the look on the face of the owner of the cottage, when he opened his front door and was confronted with the sight of a disheveled looking student pilot asking if he may use the telephone.

Needless to say, that pilot's training was immediately terminated and he was sent home to Nigeria very shortly afterwards.

There was another incident whilst I was at Perth that resulted in a student pilot having his training course terminated and him being sent home in disgrace.

The gentleman in question was from the Middle East and was a very smooth character. It was apparent that financially, he was very well off. He drove a sports car, wore expensive clothes and enjoyed socialising in bars and restaurants, which is something that he did on a very regular basis. Being tall, dark and handsome he certainly could charm the girls and would have them eating out of his hand in no time. He was a playboy. A lady's man. Or as jealous guys might say, a smooth talking, lucky bugger.

One day an instructor was flying towards Scone airfield at the end of a training session with a student. Approaching from the south east, they were just crossing the river Tay and the instructor glanced down at Errol which is a disused airfield near the northern bank of the river. To his surprise, he saw one of the school's Cessna 150 aircraft sitting on the runway at Errol. He quickly radioed the controller at Scone and asked if anyone had received a Mayday (distress) call in the last few minutes. When told that nothing had been heard on the radio, he advised them that it looked like one of the school aircraft must have experienced an engine failure, but it appeared that the pilot had made a successful forced landing at Errol.

They subsequently found out that this wasn't the case at all. Apparently, our Playboy pilot had been in a bar in Perth the night before and as usual had been hitting on a girl he fancied. During his charm offensive, he had told her he was a pilot at Scone and when she said that she would love to fly in a light aircraft, he told her 'I'll take you up tomorrow if you like.' Arrangements were then made for a friend of his to pick the girl up in his car and drive her to the disused airfield at Errol. Then Casanova, who had taken off from Scone on a solo training flight, hopped across to Errol and swooped in to land. He picked up his young girlfriend and then took her for a joyride around the local area. After landing back at Errol, he had transferred his adoring passenger to the waiting car, and his pal drove her away. However, before he could takeoff again, he was spotted by the instructor and a short while later, the whole story was revealed.

Subsequently it was rumoured that this wasn't the first time he had offered his aerial sightseeing service to an attractive girl. Whether or not that was true is not known for sure, but it was definitely the last time that he did it because he was kicked off the course and sent back home in disgrace. No doubt he was sadly missed by quite a few young girls who had been used to seeing him around the clubs and pubs of Perth.

On the 24th January 1974 Captain Rees, an examiner with the Civil Aviation Authority, awarded me a pass on my Initial instrument rating flight test. I had done it. The Civil Aviation Authority issued me with a Commercial pilot's licence and instrument rating (CPL/IR.) Licence number: 90703.

I drove away from Perth in my newly acquired Mark One Ford Capri which was loaded up with all the junk I had collected over the previous year. I was heading down to London where my Australian girlfriend was living. She was sharing a place in Barnes with a couple of other girls and we were planning a party to celebrate the fact that I had escaped from my Scottish jail. I had a long drive ahead (about 8 hours) but felt on top of the World.

My Capri was white, but had a matt black bonnet which obviously added about twenty miles an hour to it's top speed. If you were standing a couple of hundred yards away and squinted, it looked vaguely like a Ford Mustang so it goes without saying that when I was driving it, I looked the spitting image of Steve McQueen.

Eventually I arrived in London looking less like Steve McQueen and more like a Bulldog sucking a wasp. However, despite being stiff and weary, it didn't stop me from enjoying the party.

Chapter 10

My First Flying Job

As with most things in life, timing is important in aviation. That well worn phrase 'in the right place at the right time' is very applicable. I had now successfully completed the training for my Commercial Pilot's Licence and was about to start work with Dan Air, one of the leading independent airlines in Europe. They were going to put me on an in-house type rating course for the Avro 748 aircraft, so life was looking pretty damned good.

Unfortunately, one thing that wasn't so good was my timing. At the end of 1973, the 12 OPEC countries (Organisation of Arab Petroleum Exporting Countries) all agreed to stop selling oil to any nation that had supported Israel and the Yom Kippur war. The countries initially targeted were the USA, Canada, Japan, Netherlands and the U.K. The embargo had an immediate effect and over the space of just a few weeks, the price of a barrel of oil had increased by over 200%. In America, because of a weakening dollar, the price had increased by 300%. Needless to say this had a massive effect on the airline industry.

It had a massive effect on me too, because Dan Air informed me that all their planned courses had been cancelled until further notice. Until it became clear how things were going to work out regarding the oil crisis, the company was going to hold off on any expansion plans. All of a sudden, I was a pilot who's feet were staying firmly on the ground. Fortunately, a couple of months later, I got some great news from Dan Air. My conversion course onto the Avro 748 was back on.

The Avro 748 was a short haul airliner with two turbo prop Rolls Royce Dart engines, a pressurised cabin carrying 48 passengers and a crew that comprised of two pilots and two cabin attendants. It was an extremely rugged aircraft that was designed to fly multiple short sectors on a daily basis. Dan Air had introduced it on their Link City scheduled services around the U.K. in addition to scheduled services to the Channel Islands, France, Switzerland and Norway. When it first went into production in the 1960s, it was being made by the famous Avro company which by that time had been producing aircraft for more than 50 years. The Avro company morphed into Hawker Siddeley and later into British Aerospace. Consequently, over the years the aircraft's name changed from the Avro 748 to the HS 748 and then to the BAe 748. One thing that remained constant throughout all the name changes, was the fact that it was a well designed, well built and thoroughly reliable aerial workhorse.

Over the weeks that followed, I learned all about the aircraft's various systems. One person who went through that course with me became a good friend. His name was Ian Sharman and he kept saying that he couldn't believe his good fortune in getting a place

86

on the course. Ian had owned a small car repair and servicing business that was actually located on Ashford airfield in Kent. Ian had got himself a Commercial Pilot's Licence, following which he had been unable to get a flying job. Getting onto that first rung of the ladder is always tough for a newly qualified pilot. When applying for a flying job, they are frequently told to come back when they've got more experience. Of course the problem is, they can't gain that experience if nobody is prepared to give them a flying job in the first place. A classic Catch 22 situation.

Ian had continued to work in his garage, whilst constantly on the look out for a flying job. There was an airline called Skyways based at the airfield and Ian was well known to the pilots. He had an arrangement in place whereby if one of the pilots had a problem with their car, or the car merely needed servicing, they would leave the key with the on duty operations officer before they went off flying for the day. Operations would contact Ian, who would collect the key, service the car at his garage and then return the car and key to the operations office. When the pilot returned at the end of their working day, their car would be fully serviced and ready for them. Consequently Ian was a regular visitor to the Skyways office and people were used to seeing him around. They were also aware that he was a wannabe pilot.

Skyways operated a fleet of Avro 748 aircraft and was a well established airline that had been in the business for many years. However, by this time, for various reasons, they had run into financial difficulties and were on the verge of collapse. In February 1972 Dan Air stepped in and bought

87

the airline, retaining it's aircraft, flight crews and ground staff.

Fast forward now to 1974 and our planned 748 course. All the candidates for the course had been selected, but then just days before we were due to start, one of the candidates informed the company that they were dropping out. The 748 fleet manager was asked if he knew of anyone who would be interested in taking that person's place at such short notice. He immediately thought of Ian, phoned him and said 'if you can start next Monday, you've got a job.'

On Monday morning Ian was sitting in the classroom next to me with a big smile on his face. Timing is everything. Right place, right time, right result.

Having completed our ground school studies and passed the CAA examination for the type rating, the next stage was to do the base training in the aircraft itself. I was informed that Ian and I would be teamed up to do our base training together at Newcastle airport. The company booked us to fly as passengers on the Dan Air scheduled service from Bournemouth to Newcastle. Dan Air called their domestic scheduled services Link City and this particular one started in Bournemouth and then landed at Bristol, Cardiff, Manchester, Teeside and Newcastle. It picked up and dropped off passengers at each place and was a very slick, well choreographed operation.

As soon as the aircraft landed it would be taxied to the parking apron and the left hand engine shut down before the aircraft had even come to a halt. The left engine was stopped because the passenger door and the main cargo door were both on the left side of the fuselage so the sooner the prop stopped turning the better. Passenger steps were quickly moved into place and passengers who were leaving at that particular airport would get off. Passengers who were continuing on to an airport further along the route remained in their seat. Baggage handlers would unload the bags for the departing passengers and then load on the bags belonging to the joining passengers. As this was going on, the joining passengers would board and take their seats. The doors were closed and the aircraft immediately began taxiing out towards the runway. The number one engine was restarted after the aircraft was already on the move. The aircraft then took off on the next leg of it's journey. The total time from landing to taking off again was scheduled at ten minutes at each airport. It was impressive to watch and Ian and I realised that we would be expected to do that ourselves pretty soon. A daunting prospect.

Chapter 11

Flying Out of Ashford Airport

Once I had completed my line training, I was informed that I was to be based at Ashford airport in Kent. It had originally been called Lympne and had been an airfield since 1916. It had the dubious distinction of having been bombed by the Germans in both the first and second World wars.

Between the wars during the 1920s it had hosted a number of light aeroplane competitions and air races and had been the departure point for a number of long distance pioneering flights. At the start of World War Two, the Fleet Air Arm owned the airfield and in 1940 they were joined by the RAF when it became a front line fighter station. It was heavily bombed and extensively damaged by Stukas during the Battle of Britain and remained out of commission for a few months. Hawker Typhoons of Numbers 1 & 609 squadrons were based at Lympne and were later joined by a Spitfire wing.

In 1948, Silver City began a car and passenger air service to France from Lympne using Bristol Freighter aircraft. This continued until 1954 when,

One of Dan Air's Douglas DC-3 aircraft.

because the grass runways at Lympne frequently became waterlogged and unusable, the airline moved it's operation to nearby Lydd (Ferryfield) airport.

In 1956 Eric Rylands bought Lympne airfield and his airline Skyways began scheduled flights to Beauvais in France. They offered a service in which passengers could catch a coach at London Victoria, which brought them to Lympne airfield. There they would board a Skyways Douglas DC-3 that flew them to Beauvais. At Beauvais another coach transported them to the centre of Paris.

Later, Skyways Coach-Air as it was now named, ordered Avro 748 aircraft (the first airline to do so) and in March 1962, began operating them from Lympne on the coach-air service. The grass runways continued to become waterlogged and unusable at certain times of the year and it says a great deal about the rugged construction of the 748 that it was able to successfully operate in such inhospitable conditions for much of the time.

In 1965, one of the Skyways 748s (G-ARMV) crashed when landing at Lympne, which resulted in the aircraft finishing up inverted and minus one of it's wings. Amazingly, despite having a full load of passengers on board, everyone escaped serious injury. It was determined that when the aircraft had touched down heavily on it's landing gear, the nose wheels had dug into the waterlogged runway and this had flipped the aircraft onto it's back. This prompted negotiations to begin for the approval and construction of a concrete runway. Such changes are notoriously slow in coming, but eventually by early 1968 a 1,300 metre concrete runway was finally in use.

Lympne had now been renamed Ashford after the expanding town that was located a few miles away. In 1971 Skyways coach air was experiencing serious financial difficulties and a management buyout created Skyways International. This only managed to struggle on for another year and in 1972 Dan Air bought the company which they briefly branded as Dan Air Skyways. As part of the purchase, they got the 748 fleet of aircraft and scheduled service routes from Lympne to Beauvais, Clermont Ferrand and Montpellier. They also got Lympne airport.

One of the Captains based at Ashford airport was Jeff Henderson. Jeff had flown Hawker Typhoon fighters during the second world war. He was quite a character and used to cheerfully claim that he'd had the Shortest command in aviation history.

He had been a co-pilot with Skyways, flying the Douglas DC-3. Eventually the airline announced that they were going to promote him to captain and following his conversion training, the day finally dawned when he was to set off for the very first time as Captain of a DC-3. Unfortunately, when he did the pre-flight walk around inspection of the

A Dan Air Avro 748.

aircraft he failed to remove the external rudder lock. This was a simple clamping device that locked the rudder in it's central position to prevent it from swinging around in the wind when the aircraft was parked and unattended. Having got airborne despite considerable difficulty in maintaining directional control, Jeff realised what the problem was and managed to fly the aircraft around in a wide circuit using a combination of roll (using the ailerons) and yaw, by partially throttling back one of the engines to give himself asymmetric thrust. Having managed to successfully land back at the airfield, which was no mean feat in a tail-dragger with no rudder, he was immediately demoted to co-pilot again. Jeff would relate this tale and finally add 'So I was actually a captain for just 10 minutes in total'

Needless to say, the moral of his tale was to make sure you always did a careful pre-flight inspection and also checked for full and free movement of all the flight controls before takeoff.

I thoroughly enjoyed flying with Jeff. The first

time that I met him he was studying to be a barrister and started off the day by asking me 'Do you mind doing all the flying today because I've got a law exam coming up soon and I need to study?' As a brand new co-pilot, I was absolutely delighted because I wanted to get as much handling practice as possible.

On this particular day we were rostered to fly a scheduled passenger service from Ashford to Beauvais near Paris. After about forty minutes on the ground at Beauvais, we flew back to Ashford. Forty minutes later, we were off to Beauvais a second time and then back to Ashford again. The aircraft was an Avro 748 and on each flight we carried a full load of 48 passengers. So by the end of the day, I had carried one hundred and ninety two passengers, done four takeoffs and four landings, flown to Paris and back twice and thoroughly enjoyed myself.

Whilst I was doing all that, Jeff had been studiously poring over his law books. He sat his exams a few weeks later and passed with flying colours.

Amazingly, there were no serious injuries to anyone aboard this Skyways Avro 748.

Chapter 12

In the Right Place at the Right Time

Peple often talk of 'being in the right place at the right time.' I honestly can't think of a better example of this than the following: One day in August 1976, I was on a standby day, meaning that I had to make myself available at the end of a phone in case something unexpected came up, such as a pilot going sick or a diverted aircraft having thrown the flying programme into disarray. On this particular occasion, I received a call early in the morning telling me that I had to get to Gatwick as soon as possible in order to operate a flight to Cork in Ireland. Once we got to Cork, the crew were to check into a hotel for a few hours and then operate a flight back to Gatwick in the evening.

When I checked in at the Gatwick crew room later, I discovered that our aircraft had been chartered by a group of aviation enthusiasts, but nobody in the flight operations office knew any further details. Twenty minutes later, the captain, John Armitage and I were in the cockpit of our aircraft running through the pre-flight preparations and checks. In the meantime, the passengers had started boarding and one of them caught sight of me. He thought he recognised me and so asked one of the stewardesses 'Is the First Officer Bob Williams?'

When she confirmed it, he asked her if she could let me know that an ex-work colleague from BOAC was on board and would like to come up to the cockpit after takeoff to say hello. By an amazing coincidence, the guy used to work on the same shift team as me when I worked on the BOAC Boeing 707s at Heathrow. Needless to say, I was delighted to get him up into the cockpit soon after we got airborne.

We caught up on what we had both been up to since we had last met and then I asked him what today's charter was in aid of. He told me that a Shorts Sandringham flying boat had recently been flown to Southern Ireland and would be briefly based there in order to carry out a series of pleasure flights for anyone interested in buying charter tickets. The Aviation enthusiast's club that he belonged to had organised a group booking which of course also included chartering our aircraft to take them to and from Ireland. The guy who had organised it all was on board, so we invited him up front to tell us more.

He explained that the aircraft owner and operator was Antilles Air Boats who were based in St. Croix in the U.S. Virgin Islands. They had brought the aircraft over to Ireland to carry out a series of 'pleasure flights' throughout the summer of 1976. Our passengers had arranged to be taken on one of those flights and that was where we were now headed. During this conversation, I told the charter organiser that I was very envious that he was going to fly on such an iconic aircraft. He responded by saying that we could come along as well if we wanted because they had some spare seats aboard the seaplane. John decided that he would rather stay at Cork in the hotel, but that he was quite happy for me to go. Needless to say I gratefully accepted the offer.

After landing at Cork, we travelled by coach to the lake we would be departing from and shortly after getting there, we heard the distinctive sound of powerful piston engines overhead. The aircraft made a graceful curved approach and landing and then, as it taxied back closer to the shore, two flags were placed into position above the aircraft's cockpit windows. The American Stars and Stripes and the Antilles air boats company logo. Then a hatch in the nose section of the aircraft opened up. A man's head and shoulders appeared in the open hatch and he threw out a sea anchor. This was going to be very special indeed!

We were all taken out to the aircraft about a dozen at a time in small boats equipped with an outboard motor. As we pulled alongside the open forward boarding door of the aircraft, we were greeted by the Captain and a Stewardess. The Captain was none other than Charles F. Blair. The stewardess was none other than his lovely wife, the former Hollywood actress Maureen O'Hara.

Charles Blair was an amazing aviator. Born in 1909, he flew for the U.S. Navy way back in 1932 and was then a mail pilot with United in 1933. As chief pilot of American Overseas Airlines, he flew survey flights to the U.K., Africa and South America. He flew the first ever non stop commercial flight across the Atlantic in a Sikorsky flying boat and then during World War Two, flew for air transport command in addition to being a test pilot for Grumman, testing Naval fighters and flying boats.

After the war, he carried out the first trans

Atlantic proving flights on Lockheed Constellations and Boeing Stratocruisers on behalf of American Overseas Airlines. At the same time, he ran his own airline, operating a C-46 Commando on charters flights from New York to Europe and South America. In 1950, he approached the USAF looking to borrow a P-51 Mustang for some 'special flights' he had been planning. They refused on the grounds that the flights were too risky. His solution was to buy his own P-51, modify it with a 1,650 hp Merlin engine and fit it with long range fuel tanks.

On 31st January 1951, he flew his aircraft from New York to London Heathrow to test the effects of jet streams. Having found a jet stream at 37,000 feet, he covered the 3,022 nautical miles at an average speed of 388 knots. The flight took 7 hours 48 minutes, making it the fastest crossing of the Atlantic in a single piston engine aircraft. That record still stood over seventy years later.

Later that same year, he flew his P-51 from Bardufoss (Norway) to Fairbanks (Alaska) in what was the first solo flight over the North Pole and the first flight over the pole in a single engine aircraft. The following year, he was awarded the Harmon International Aviation Award "The World's outstanding aviator.' In 1959 he was made a Brigadier-General in the USAF and went on to make numerous supersonic flights in the USAF fighter wing. He worked in the development of low level navigation and weapons delivery techniques and he won the Thurlow award for his outstanding contribution to the science of navigation.

In 1959, he won the Distinguished Flying Cross for leading a formation of fighters on a trans-polar flight that required mid air refuelling three times en route. In 1962 he joined NASA as a consultant on navigation and, at the same time remained a pilot with Pan Am, operating a number of round the World schedules on the Boeing 707. In 1968 he married the Hollywood actress Maureen O'Hara. He retired from Pan Am to start his own airline Antilles Air Boats. This airline was based in St. Croix in the U.S. Virgin Islands and started up using Grumman Goose aircraft. He later bought two Short Sandringham aircraft and by the time that I met him, the airline was flying 23 amphibian aircraft, making it the largest sea plane airline in the World. They operated 120 flights per day around the Caribbean. After 46 years as a pilot Blair logged over 45,000 flying hours and completed 1,575 Atlantic crossings.

So, with Captain Blair in command, I climbed aboard the Sandringham and we took off for a flight following the coast around the southern end of Ireland. We flew at 1,500 feet on a lovely clear day. It was absolutely magical. On board, it felt more like a ship than an aircraft and weight saving was nowhere in evidence. It was built like the proverbial outhouse. When I visited the toilet during the flight, I was confronted by a huge porcelain throne with a solid wooden seat. The enormous wash basin was also made of Porcelain and had large chrome taps. Back in the cabin, the reading light above my seat had a fluted glass shade and a sturdy brass switch to operate it. In terms of aviation, it was like nothing I had ever come across before. Something from a bygone age.

Staring out of the large window by my seat, listening to the radial engines droning away it was easy to imagine a time long ago when passengers set off in a seaplane just like this one, in order to travel to some far off destination, stopping off at exotic places en route. A time when getting there was just as exciting

Captain Charles Blair. President and owner of Antilles Air Boats.

and enjoyable as arriving. All the passengers today of course, were the enthusiasts that I had brought over from London and they had been excitedly taking it in turns to visit the cockpit. When it looked as though everyone had made the visit, I went in myself. The two pilots were seated at their controls, whilst the flight engineer, who did of course have his own seat, was wearing a headset with an enormous coiled lead that was long enough to allow him to wander freely around the cockpit area.

I spoke to him briefly asking about the aircraft's performance in terms of fuel consumption and endurance and so on and asked him about the trans Atlantic flight they had made from the Virgin Isles to Ireland. I then moved forward and introduced myself to Captain Blair who asked me what type of aircraft I had brought his passengers over in from London. We talked a little about flying generally and at one point I asked him about a porpoising motion I had noticed during our takeoff run. I had

The Sandringham was a civilian version of the Sunderland Maritime patrol/anti-submarine bomber. It carried 45 passengers, was powered by four Pratt & Whitney twin wasp engines, cruised at around 180 knots and had an impressive endurance of approximately 14 hours.

wondered if it was a manoeuvre that was required to get the aircraft to break free of the water. I'd already told him that flying in a seaplane was a completely new experience for me and not something that I knew anything about. He told me that the water had been completely calm when we went to takeoff. Apparently, when the water is glassy smooth like that, it is difficult to get the aircraft up 'onto the step' (whereupon it is aquaplaning on just the lower part of the hull). The porpoising action I detected was him see-sawing the elevators to try and get us up on the step. In the end, he was forced to bring the aircraft right around in a large arc so that we ran back through our own wake. The waves we had created in our wake did the trick and we skipped up onto the narrow lower hull section, allowing us to get up to flying speed and take to the air. I found the whole experience really fascinating and loved every minute of it. It really was an amazing experience and a day to remember.

On the second of September 1978, Blair was flying a Grumman Goose from St. Croix to St. Thomas in the Virgin Isles. One of the aircraft's engines seized and blew it's cowlings off. With the increased drag caused by the loss of the cowlings, the aircraft was unable to maintain altitude on its one remaining engine. Blair tried to fly the aircraft in ground effect about 20 feet above the water, but the aircraft struck the water and cartwheeled in around it's left wing. Charles Blair and three of the ten passengers aboard were killed. At the time of his death, 69 year old Charles Blair had amassed an incredible 45,000 flying hours.

Years after taking that flight in the Sandringham, I found myself working for an airline based at London Heathrow. Our offices were in the Queens Building and during an early visit there, I was walking along a corridor, when I came across a small plaque next to a window. Behind the window was a model of a bright red P-51 Mustang mounted on a pedestal. The plaque commemorated Charles Blair's record breaking flight from New York to Heathrow in his Mustang. From then on, I always made a point of giving Captain Blair's commemorative plaque a nod of appreciation every time I walked past.

Chapter 13

All We Need Is a Small Rubber 'O' Ring

At one time, I worked with a person who had been a Flight Engineer on the de Havilland Comet. He later retrained to become a pilot and that is when our paths crossed. To say that he was a character would be an understatement and he was constantly getting into trouble with the management for stepping out of line in one way or another. Despite his reputation for being 'trouble' I found him to be a likeable rogue and he had a terrific sense of humour. As a raconteur he was up there with the best and his stories frequently had us in fits of laughter. One such story that sticks in my mind, tells of him operating as a flight engineer on a trip in a Comet. Having flown to an overseas destination, he was doing a pre-departure walk-around of the aircraft before setting off on the return journey. He then discovered a leaking joint on part of the hydraulic system. Having dismantled the joint, he realised that the leak was due to a rubber 'O' ring seal having perished. This of course was an easy fix, except for one thing. He didn't have a replacement rubber 'O' ring to hand. Frustrated that their departure was going to be prevented by something as simple as a small rubber seal, he searched for an answer. His captain hadn't been slow in voicing his own frustration and had expressed disappointment that Dave had been unable to resolve the situation. Shortly afterwards, Dave proudly announced that he had fixed the problem. Having tested and confirmed the efficiency of his repair, passengers were boarded and the flight departed.

When the aircraft was in the cruise and the workload had consequently dropped, Dave started to fill in the technical log. This very substantial manual contained copious amounts of data relating to the aircraft, its serviceability status, details of any defects that had arisen or indeed still existed, along with the recording of takeoff time, landing time and details of the departure and arrival fuel quantities. The flight engineer was responsible for recording all this data and the captain, having checked it was correct, finally signed each page to show his satisfaction and acceptance of the content. The Captain looked over his shoulder at Dave who was seated to his right and slightly behind him. He could see that he had completed the section of the technical log that called for a description of the nature of the defect and the subsequent remedial action.

However, Dave now had his pen hovering above a section of the page that asked for the part number/ serial number of the item that had been fitted in order to rectify the defect.

"What seems to be the difficulty there Dave" he asked. "

"Umm... Oh wait, I know what to do."

With that, he delved into his pocket, pulled out an item, glanced at it for a moment and then returned to his technical logbook. Having completed his page entry, he passed the log across to his Captain for approval. The Captain studied the entry for a moment and then turned to his engineer.

"Can I please see the item that you took from your pocket a moment a go?" The item was duly handed over. It was a packet of condoms. The captain studied the packet of condoms and then the page of the technical log. He noted that Dave had filled in the section calling for a part number with the British Standards number printed on the condom packet.

He turned to Dave and said "Do you mean to tell me that we are bringing this aircraft home thanks to a British Standards approved condom?"

Dave replied with a simple 'Correct.' The captain signed the log and handed it back without a word.

Chapter 14

Rain Repellent

I had been a pilot on the Boeing 737 for some time before I actually got around to using one particular feature on the aircraft. There were two push buttons on the overhead panel that activated rain repellent. Just forward of each pilot's front windscreen, there was a spray nozzle much like the windscreen washer on a car. By pressing a button on the overhead panel in the flight deck, a pilot could cause a measured amount of liquid to squirt onto their windscreen. This magic liquid was actually called 'RainBoe' (as it was licensed to the Boeing company). It was actually a very effective rain repellent and did an amazing job of suddenly clearing a screen when it had previously been blurred by torrential rain. Under normal circumstances, the windscreen wipers were perfectly adequate, but in very heavy rain, a quick squirt of the magic rain repellent rapidly improved the situation. There was a drawback unfortunately. If you accidentally squirted the magic liquid onto a DRY windscreen, it would become covered in a semi-opaque film that was seemingly impossible to remove. Was this a common problem though? Yes it was.

The switches to activate the rain repellent were located close to the cabin crew call button. Imagine the following situation: The aircraft is sitting on the ground prior to departure and two pilots are relaxed with all necessary tasks completed. There is a lull in proceedings and one pilot turns to the other:

"Do you fancy a coffee?"

The other pilot replies "Good idea."

In this relaxed and laid back atmosphere, the first pilot reaches up to press the cabin crew call button. Unfortunately, they hit the rain repellent button by mistake. A generous dose of RainBoe is now deposited onto the windscreen. Yet another aircraft's windscreen is smeared with the apparently immovable film of RainBoe. What to do?

This scenario occurred so frequently that Boeing

The cockpit of a de Havilland Comet. I was once lucky enough to take a flight seated in the cockpit of a Comet. Some years later, when I was at Dan Air's training centre at Horsham, I had the pleasure of flying their Comet simulator a few times. The simulator engineers generously allowed me to fly it when it wasn't being used by the Comet crews.

had a whole team of people searching for a magic formula that would remove their RainBoe from a dry windscreen. Much money and valuable time was spent testing various concoctions and then, one of the researchers accidentally spilled his can of Coca Cola onto the test screen. It miraculously cleared! A notice was subsequently circulated to let everyone know of this unexpected result and we used Coke thereafter! Years later, it was discovered that RainBoe was carcinogenic so it was quickly removed from the flight deck. It had formerly been located on the bulkhead directly behind the captain's seat so I certainly wasn't sorry to see it removed.

The idea of a whole department of people working on a solution to remove RainBoe from a dry aircraft windscreen puts me in mind of a story of the National Aeronautics and Space Administration (NASA) spending loads of money to develop a pen that worked in a zero gravity environment. The story goes that one of their guys asked their Russian counterpart what his agency had done regarding that particular problem. He answered that they issued their Cosmonauts with pencils. Probably not true, but I love the story anyway.

Chapter 15

Flying from Aberdeen for the Oil Industry

North Sea oil exploration in the early seventies had revealed enormous potential in the region, as a result of which Aberdeen airport quickly became incredibly busy. The expansion in both fixed wing and rotary wing air traffic was enormous. Soon, Aberdeen was handling more helicopter traffic than any other airport in the World. My employer (Dan Air) was just one of many fixed wing operators there and with the huge increase in air traffic, the number of airline personnel at the airport increased proportionally. As a temporary solution, a Portacabin village had sprung up to accommodate them. During periods of rain, it sat in a sea of mud. In the depths of winter, you would trudge through the mud leaning your body at an angle to fight against the wind. Upon reaching Dan Air's cabin, you would wrench the door open and as you entered the building there would be a shout to 'shut that bloody door!' Slamming the door behind you, the howling wind suddenly stopped and you nearly fell over before realising that you no longer had to lean your body at an angle in order to stay in the same place. I also remember that the place had a strong smell of paraffin from the room heaters, but at least it was warm.

If the weather was expected to be bad in the Shetlands (usually a fair assumption) and we had been unable to get any current weather reports from the Met office, we had a cunning but unofficial way of getting an update on the weather conditions.

On the southern tip of the mainland of Shetland, is the Sumburgh Head lighthouse. You pass close to it when on left base for an approach onto runway 33 at Sumburgh airport. In the past, a number of us had taken a walk up to the lighthouse when in between flights and the lighthouse keeper was a pleasant character who was always very welcoming. He was of course very familiar with the changing weather conditions in the Shetland Isles so was as good a weather observer as you could ever wish to meet. When we were at the top of his lighthouse he pointed out certain landmarks at varying distances that were a good guide to the prevailing visibility. Consequently, if we were at Aberdeen airport, planning a flight to Sumburgh and were unable to get any official weather information, a phone call to the lighthouse keeper soon gave us a damned good idea of what to expect. On the basis of his report, we decided whether or not we should give it a go.

I should point out that we always carried round trip fuel when departing Aberdeen, so if the weather at Sumburgh turned out to be so bad that we couldn't land there, we would merely fly back to Aberdeen.

On the 11th of February 1977, I operated my last flight on the Avro 748. I had clocked up 1,558 hours on the type. During that time, I completed 1,914 takeoffs and landings. It's always a good sign when the number of takeoffs you've completed is the same as the number of landings. It means that you must be doing something right.

On reflection, the 748 was an excellent aircraft on which to gain experience. Lots of hand flying (autopilots are for softies!) All the aircraft systems were manually operated and things like the pressurisation system were quite crude and had to be nursed carefully. Gentle movement of the dump valve lever and gradual manual operation of the spill valves was necessary to ensure everyone's eardrums remained intact. Those controls were on the First Officer's side of the cockpit and out of reach of the Captain. Of course this also meant that you could spitefully whack the dump valve open if the Captain had previously given you a hard time !

The 748 was a really rugged and reliable aircraft and those Rolls Royce Dart turboprop engines were absolutely bulletproof. Mind you, their loud and distinctive high pitched scream caused widespread deafness to airport personnel around the World.

Chapter 16

The Painful Birth of the BAC1-11

The BAC 1-11 was a revolutionary aircraft when it first arrived on the scene. It had initially been designed as a 'bus stop jet.' The idea was that it would operate lots of short flights each day and have the ability to be turned around rapidly between each flight. In order to achieve that, it had to be designed to be as self-sufficient as possible. Anyone who has been involved with airline operations knows only too well that when an aircraft arrives at an airport, the ideal scenario is to get the passengers off as quickly as possible, and then board the passengers for the next flight and get the aircraft on its way again. However, simple and frustrating things often impede this process. For example, once the aircraft has arrived at the parking spot, it needs an alternative electrical supply (a Ground Power Unit) to be put into place before the engines can be shut down. If the aircraft is on a remote parking stand, passenger steps have to be brought out and wheeled into position. Alternatively, If it is on an air bridge, then there is a delay whilst the air bridge operator manoeuvres the whole thing into position alongside the passenger doorway. Once the passengers from the inbound flight have got off and those for the outbound flight have boarded, the steps must be removed. To start the aircraft's engines, an air start unit must be connected into position. This supplies the air needed to spin up the jet engines as part of the starting process.

Once the engines are running, both the air starter unit and the ground power unit must be disconnected. If the aircraft was on an air bridge, then a towbar has to be connected to the aircraft's nose gear leg and the aircraft pushed back by a tug vehicle. All this takes time and of course it also assumes that the airport authorities do actually have all the necessary ground equipment available for use at the exact time that you need it. When designing the BAC 1-11, they wanted to ensure the aircraft wasn't dependent on any of this specialised ground equipment. To achieve this, they fitted it with the following:

1. An Auxiliary Power Unit (APU). This is basically a small jet engine that has it's own electrical generator. It is not only capable of powering all the aircraft's electrical systems, but can also provide air conditioning for the passenger cabin and cockpit. When the time comes to start the aircraft's engines, the APU can then supply the air needed for that process.
2. To enable passengers to disembark and board the aircraft, the 1-11 had integral steps called air-stairs at both the front and rear doors. These could be quickly lowered and raised by the cabin crew and enabled them to get passengers on and off whenever it suited them.
3. The two cargo holds had access doors with

their lower sills set at waist level for baggage handlers working at ground level. There was therefore no need for any ladders or platforms to be put into place, because they were able to load the cargo compartments from ground level.

These were just some of the innovative features that were incorporated into the initial design of the BAC 1-11. However, one of the most significant design features was to be found in the cockpit. Jet airliners such as the de Havilland Comet, Boeing 707, Douglas DC-8 and Boeing 727 all had a minimum of three crew members up front. Namely, two pilots and a flight engineer.

Sometimes referred to as 'two flying and one on the panel.' The one on the panel was looking after the aircraft's systems such as fuel, electrics, hydraulics, air conditioning and pressurisation. The other two people concentrated on flying the aircraft. Now however, the cockpit and all the systems on the 1-11 were designed to be operated by just two pilots.

It is difficult to emphasise just how controversial it was at the time to try and introduce a jet airliner into the world, if it had just two pilots running the show. How could you possibly do away with the valuable contribution afforded by a flight engineer, when that person's presence had always been considered absolutely vital on jet airliners before?

The designers of the BAC 1-11 wanted to ensure that the cockpit was laid out in such a way that all vital controls for operating the aircraft were within easy reach of both pilots. The systems panel that would normally be operated by a flight engineer was now mounted on an overhead panel which was accessible to both pilots. It's ergonomic design, plus a certain degree of automation would ensure that everything could be managed by just two people.

The systems were designed with a great deal of built-in redundancy for safety. The hydraulic system for example powered so many vital services that is was designed with two separate reservoirs, two engine driven hydraulic pumps and two electric auxiliary pumps. In other words, a lot of built-in redundancy and backups.

The ailerons were operated by means of servo tabs and although the elevators and rudder were hydraulically powered, there were mechanical linkages to them should hydraulic pressure be completely lost.

The electrical system was a constant frequency AC system. There were two generators driven by engine mounted constant speed drive and starter units, plus an APU generator that was capable of supplying the whole system. There was a battery to start the APU and to provide standby DC power plus a static inverter which provided AC power for the essential services.

The airframe design itself, was built using the fail-safe principle. This meant that in the unlikely event that a single structural member failed, the strength of the structure as a whole would not be reduced below what was required to sustain normal flight loads. This is a roundabout way of saying that the airframe was built like the proverbial brick outhouse. Panels at the wing joints were actually machined from the solid and the whole aircraft was 'over engineered.' The corrosion inhibitive processes used during manufacture were also revolutionary and cutting edge for the time, to ensure there would be no deterioration during in service use.

The managing director of British United Airways at this time was Freddie Laker. He was a good friend of Geoff Knight, who was the marketing director for the British Aircraft Corporation.

Laker told him that his airline was looking to replace their Viscount fleet of aircraft and he outlined the performance requirements for any potential replacement aircraft. Satisfied that the proposed BAC 1-11 design was going to fit the bill, in 1961 British United Airways placed an order for 10 of the new aircraft, with an option to purchase a further 5. With this announcement, Laker's airline (BUA) became the launch customer for the new type. Meanwhile, absolutely nothing was heard from the state airline (BEA).

In the recent past, British aircraft manufacturers had allowed their proposed designs to be heavily influenced by the two British state airlines BEA and BOAC. The Vickers VC10, whilst undoubtedly a fine aircraft had morphed into a type that had been designed specifically to satisfy the needs of BOAC to operate in and out of short runways and 'hot and high' airfields such as Nairobi (5,327 feet above mean sea level). Whilst the aircraft did indeed satisfy this performance requirement, it did so at the expense of operating economy. It's power to weight ratio, combined with a sophisticated wing design gave it excellent takeoff capability, but it was too fuel thirsty in the cruise to be economical when compared to other long haul aircraft such as the Boeing 707.

Consequently, it did not appeal to the world's airlines who's accountants merely looked upon it as a gas guzzler. Whilst those passengers who had flown on it, absolutely loved the VC-10, it isn't the travelling public that chooses what aircraft type an airline buys. Instead, it is the Accountants. The VC-10 did not sell well and when airport authorities around the World began extending existing runways and building new airports with longer runways, there was little need for the VC-10's superior runway performance. BOAC, who had been so involved in the aircraft's original specification, were so loudly and publicly critical of it's operating costs, that they managed to wheedle a £30 million payment from the government as recompense for operating the type. They then promptly sold some VC-10s to Boeing as part of a deal to buy more Boeing 707s! Boeing immediately scrapped the VC-10s they had purchased because they didn't want them to be sold on to airlines that might otherwise buy their product. The message that this sent out to the airlines of the world was effectively 'If Britain's National airline doesn't even want the VC-10, then neither do we.' The effect on sales was inevitably disastrous. In the end, a total of just 54 VC-10s were built. By comparison, 865 Boeing 707s were built.

The Trident design was similarly messed with by British European Airways (BEA) Originally conceived by the de Havilland company, which was later absorbed into Hawke Siddeley, the initial design of the Trident called for a much bigger aircraft with a greater payload and range capability. To enable it to use relatively short runways, it was also required to have impressive takeoff and landing performance. As this was clearly going to be a brand new and radical design, the British manufacturer initially felt that they needed to join forces with another established aircraft manufacturer in order to share the design and development costs. The American company Boeing was approached and the two companies began discussions. Boeing were immediately impressed with the design proposal and expressed an interest in going ahead with a joint venture.

Unfortunately, the British company then revealed their proposed design to BEA, who said the aircraft would not suit their needs for two main reasons.

- They couldn't imagine ever needing to carry that many passengers, so felt the aircraft should be made significantly smaller.
- They felt the aircraft's range capability should also be reduced because none of BEA's destinations required it to fly particularly far.

Sadly, Hawker Siddeley allowed themselves to be swayed by these arguments and the design was altered to accommodate fewer passengers and to carry them over a shorter distance. Because the aircraft was to be made smaller, the engines that had originally been proposed were replaced by the less powerful Rolls Royce Spey engines. Boeing was unimpressed with the revised design and walked away from the deal.

Once the Trident had been built, it didn't take long before BEA decided that the Trident they had asked for wasn't big enough and it needed to carry more passengers! So it was made bigger, which was a good thing, but that made it heavier, which was a bad thing. This resulted in the takeoff performance being severely degraded. In fact the aircraft quickly gained the nickname 'the ground gripper' and some cynical people claimed that it only got airborne because of the curvature of the Earth. In a later variant, they even had to add a small additional (fourth) engine in order to give it enough oomph to get airborne from certain airfields such as Gibraltar.

Unsurprisingly, the type didn't sell in great numbers and a total of just 117 were built. Meanwhile, Boeing had decided to forge ahead and build an aircraft that closely followed the original design they had been shown by the British manufacturer. In other words, one that carried more passengers over a greater distance. They called it the Boeing 727 and they built a total of 1,832.

Having got their fingers burned by building aircraft that satisfied the needs of the two national airlines, but didn't really appeal to anyone else, the manufacturer was determined not to make the same mistake with the BAC 1-11. It was to appeal to as many airlines as possible and with that in mind, they embarked on a worldwide fact finding tour. They visited 89 different airlines and engaged in detailed discussions to discover exactly what those potential customers were looking for in a brand new aircraft design. The result was that 60 airlines immediately expressed an interest in the project. What was particularly exciting for the British sales team, was that a number of American Airlines said they wanted the aircraft. Braniff, Eastern, Frontier, Mohawk and Ozark all stated that they intended to buy the 1-11. This really made the U.S. Civil Aeronautics Bureau sit up and take notice. In a blatant protectionist move, they announced that they were going to block the sales on the grounds that American Airlines should be forced to buy American built aircraft.

Braniff refused to be intimidated by this action and went ahead with their order, as did Mohawk. Then in 1963, American Airlines stepped forward and put in a significant order, whilst simultaneously making it clear that they would almost certainly be looking for a lot more in the near future. This was a bitter blow for the American Douglas company, who had just announced their intention to build the DC-9 to rival the BAC 1-11.

At this stage, it was estimated that the British jet had a two year lead on the DC-9. Clearly the BAC 1-11 was off to a fantastic start in terms of orders, but now it was necessary to get the aircraft built, test flown and certified by the World's aviation authorities.

A very rigorous and extensive flight test programme was mapped out. Jock Bryce was appointed chief test pilot for the project and Mike Lithgow was appointed deputy chief test pilot. Unfortunately, it was all about to go disastrously wrong.

On the 28th of July 1963, the prototype BAC 1-11 was rolled out of the production hangar at Hurn airport. By way of saying thank you to British United for being the first airline to show faith in the project by placing an order, the prototype had been painted in the airline's colours and signage.

The flying programme began at an impressive pace with the prototype clocking up over 50 flights in two months. Then, disaster struck. On the 22nd of October 1963, it took off with Mike Lithgow and Dick Rymer at the controls. They were accompanied by five flight test observers and the purpose of this particular flight was to further explore the aircraft's stall characteristics. The aircraft had been stalled a number of times on previous flights and on this particular flight it carried out four stalls without difficulty or incident. However, when the aircraft entered a stall for the fifth time, as it experienced the sudden loss of lift, followed by a downward acceleration, it began to pitch up rapidly. This increase in incidence caused the elevators to trail upwards and although Lithgow pushed forward on his control column, the elevator servo tab had insufficient authority to move the trailing elevator surfaces down. The aircraft was locked into an irrecoverable deep stall. In an attempt to alter their predicament, the pilots continued to make numerous control inputs in roll and yaw whilst simultaneously varying the engine thrust. It was all to no avail and with the aircraft descending at a rate of 10,000 feet per minute, it crashed into open ground at Chicklade, Wiltshire and was completely destroyed. Needless to say, none of the seven occupants survived.

The Air Accident Investigation Branch (AAIB) reported their findings as soon as they had completed their meticulous work searching for the cause of the crash. They listed a number of findings, the most significant of which pointed to the design of the elevators, which were operated aerodynamically by servo tabs. Movement of the control column by the pilot would actually move a servo tab, which would then cause the elevator surface to be moved aerodynamically in the opposite direction. In the accident aircraft it had become blatantly clear that the tab had insufficient authority to move the elevator as much as was needed when the aircraft was in a stalled condition. BAC responded by incorporating a mechanical linkage between the cockpit control columns and the elevators. They also altered the shape of the wing's leading edge to encourage a pitch down movement of the aircraft as the wing stalled. Soon after the test flying programme resumed, the chief test pilot Jock Bryce, failed his medical renewal and consequently lost his pilot's licence.

Brian Trubshaw was brought in to takeover as chief test pilot. Once he had assessed the handling characteristics of the aircraft for himself, he was reportedly unimpressed and expressed concern over the elevator controls and how the aircraft handled in pitch.

Just over four months after the loss of the prototype, the replacement test aircraft, G-ASJB, suffered a bounced landing following which it struck the runway so hard that the landing gear collapsed and the left engine ended up almost completely detached from the airframe. It was subsequently deemed a write-off and was scrapped. Difficulty with the manual elevator controls was again felt to have contributed to the accident. The flying programme was suspended pending further investigations and modifications.

Another aircraft, G-ASJD had been chosen as the aircraft that was to recommence low-speed handling trials. It had been modified with altered wing leading edges, inboard wing fences and powered elevators rather than the servo tab design. By now, a year had passed since the prototype had first taken to the air and now Juliet Delta took off to carry out some stall tests.

The handling pilot was Peter Baker, a former test pilot with Handley Page and now part of the 1-11 test team. Upon entering a stall, the aircraft didn't respond correctly when Baker pushed forward on the control column to lower the nose. He concluded that the aircraft must have entered a stable stall, so he deployed the tail parachute that had been fitted to this aircraft specifically for such an eventuality. However, this did nothing to improve the situation and the aircraft's rate of descent increased to 6,000 feet per minute. In desperation, Baker selected full thrust on the engines whilst simultaneously selecting full flap. This had the effect of reducing the rate of descent to 1,000 feet per minute. The aircraft was over some open Army ranges on the Salisbury Plain and Baker was able to make a wheels-up forced landing onto the grass. The occupants were fine and although the aircraft had suffered quite substantial damage to the lower fuselage, it was later transported to Hurn and repaired.

Unsurprisingly, the three crashes had a detrimental effect on sales. A number of airline customers who had expressed an interest suddenly changed their mind and walked away. Even though the remainder of the test programme was completed without any major snags along the way, the whole process was (understandably) carried out very slowly and deliberately. What this meant of course, is that the two year lead over the Douglas DC-9 that the 1-11 had previously enjoyed, disappeared fast.

The 1-11 test programme took 20 months from first flight to entering airline service. By comparison, the DC-9 went through the same process in just 8 months. The BAC 1-11 received it's Certificate of Airworthiness on the 5th April 1965. The Douglas DC-9 got it's Certificate of Airworthiness on the 23rd November 1965.

Once the 1-11 finally entered airline service it quickly proved to be a very fine aircraft and went on to become the most successful British jet in terms of Worldwide sales. Eventually, 244 aircraft were built before production ceased. The aircraft continued in airline service all around the World for decades and although the airframe had an approved life of 85,000 flying hours or landings, it was the noisy Rolls Royce

Spey engines that finally forced airlines to stop operating the type. Even with 'hush kits' fitted to the engine, it was unable to meet Stage 3 noise limits without significant weight/range reductions.

There were proposals to re-engine the aircraft using the more powerful and significantly quieter Rolls Royce Tay engine and the Dee Howard Corporation of America actually tested and demonstrated a Tay powered 1-11 very impressively. Unfortunately Dee Howard failed to achieve sufficient interest or support to continue with the project.

It should be mentioned that BAC themselves were reluctant to encourage the development of a Tay powered 1-11 because they were busy promoting their 146 aircraft and didn't want to harm potential sales of that type by introducing an improved 1-11. That apparent conflict of interest must surely have influenced them to dismiss the project.

With reference to the BAC 1-11's legendary 'over-engineered' build quality, here is a remarkable example:A 401 series aircraft was built for American Airlines and made it's first flight on the 6th December 1966. It was subsequently sold to Dan Air (at which time it was re-registered G-AXCK) and I flew it many times when I was working for that airline. The aircraft was again sold on and it's final owner was the Northrop Grumman company in America. They used it as an airborne test bed to evaluate Military radar and avionics equipment. It made it's last flight on the 7th May 2019, which was in fact the last time that any BAC 1-11 flew. That aircraft's first flight and last flight were separated by a remarkable 52 years and 5 months.

Chapter 17

Technical Problems Down Route

One tremendous thing about flying the 1-11s in Dan Air was the variety of work and the amazing number of destinations that we flew to. If, as the old saying goes, variety is the spice of life, then we certainly had plenty of spice in our lives. By consulting my logbooks I can see that I flew to 120 different airfields in that aircraft.

Like the majority of airlines, when we flew to an airport in another country, we didn't have any company engineers to greet us and help out in the event of any technical problems. All the Dan Air pilots were trained to self-manage a turnaround away from base. Consequently, we would carry out the pre-flight inspection of the aircraft, check and if necessary top up the engine oil (we carried cans and an oil pump in the hold) top up the hydraulic fluid (again, we carried that in the hold) and set up and oversee the refuelling of the aircraft. As part of our initial conversion course, we had all been shown how to do these things by the ground engineers. Most of the time, our turnarounds went without a hitch, but occasionally something unusual would crop up.

I remember the first time that I encountered a problem down route. We had flown out from Gatwick to Malaga and I was now doing my walk around inspection of the aircraft in preparation for the return flight to England. A few moments before, I had spoken to the guy operating the fuel truck and had set up the refuel panel to the amounts I needed in each tank. Everything was going well. Just then, a baggage handler came up to me and said in broken English 'is a big problem signor.' I followed him as he beckoned me towards the rear of the aircraft and then, as he held his arm out and pointed, I stared at the aircraft's rear cargo door. It wasn't attached to the aircraft anymore. It was lying on the ground. With experience, I later discovered that this wasn't an isolated occurrence. The forward and rear cargo doors were designed so that when you opened them, they slid smoothly on their runners, down and out of the way of the cargo access hatch.

This made life easier for the cargo handlers to load or unload items through the waist- high hatch. Unfortunately, if a baggage handler operated the door opening handle and then just allowed the door to drop down the runners under it's own considerable weight, it sometimes jumped over the door stops, shot off the end of the runners and clattered onto the tarmac. It took a number of people a great deal of heaving, straining and swearing to wrestle the door back onto the runners once again. You generally ended up bathed in sweat, covered in grease and with grazed knuckles for your trouble. At one particular airport, the baggage handlers all seemed Hell bent on flinging the doors open with such force that disaster was pretty much guaranteed. It happened often enough that we had to issue an instruction that they weren't to operate the doors at all. Instead they had to wait for one of the pilots to come down and operate them smoothly and gently. It may be my imagination, but it always seemed to be pouring with rain whenever I had to go out and open or close the cargo doors!

A problem that occasionally cropped up on the 1-11, was a 'stuck' valve in the pneumatic system preventing you from being able to start an engine. The engines were attached to the fuselage of the aircraft by a stub wing and a valve housed within that structure sometimes got stuck in the closed position. Normally, to start an engine, the pilot would select the appropriate switches on the overhead panel in the flight deck. Then, air from the APU (Auxiliary Power Unit) would pass along pneumatic ducting and a valve in the stub wing would open to allow it to pass through to the engine. As the engine was spun up by this APU air, the pilot would open the HP fuel cock to direct fuel into the combustion chamber, Igniters would then ignite the fuel air mixture and your engine started. Except sometimes it didn't because the valve refused to open.

We carried a special tool in the flight deck for just such an eventuality. It was a long Tommy bar on the end of which was a socket spanner. By opening a small access panel on the underside of the stub wing, you could feed the extension bar in and open the stuck valve manually.

To start the engine in this way, we had a well rehearsed procedure which went as follows:

1. Attempt to start the engines in the normal way.
2. Discover that the inlet valve has failed to open and is stuck.

3. Utter a few swear words.
4. Remove a coin from your pocket and say to your colleague 'Heads or Tails?'
5. Toss the coin. The loser has to manually open the valve.
6. Assuming you are the loser, collect the special tool from it's stowage and now walk the full length of the passenger cabin down to the rear ventral door. Lower the Airstairs and go outside.
7. Open the access panel in the stub wing, feed in the socket spanner and attach it to the valve.
8. Manually crank open the valve and hold it in the open position.
9. Give a thumbs up signal to the stewardess who is standing at the top of the Airstairs.
10. They now turn and give a thumbs up signal to another stewardess who is stationed at the front end of the passenger cabin.
11. This person steps into the flight deck and says to the pilot 'Okay to start.'
12. The pilot initiates the start sequence. In the meantime, you continue to hold the valve in the open position with the tool. The engine (which is just a couple of feet away from you) starts to spin up. Fuel is pumped in, igniters come on and the engine roars into life.
13. Once the engine has reached self sustaining speed, the pilot in the flight deck gives the forward stewardess a thumbs up signal.They repeat the signal to the stewardess at the rear of the aircraft.
14. She now signals to you that it is okay to release the valve and remove the tool.
15. With the engine now screaming away right

next to your ear, you remove the tool, close the access panel, climb the stairs, close the rear cabin door.

16. By now, 119 passengers are looking towards the rear of the cabin and staring worriedly straight at you.

17. Avoiding eye contact, you ignore their worried stares, walk the full length of the cabin and return to the flight deck.

18. You hope like hell that the valve for the other engine doesn't need to be similarly persuaded.

I remember one occasion when that manual start sequence didn't quite go to plan. We had operated a night flight from London Gatwick to Palma airport on the island of Majorca. We were now about to set off for the flight back to Gatwick. When we tried to start number two engine, nothing happened.

Having lost the 'heads or tails' call, it was down to me to go outside. When we were ready I manually cranked open the offending valve. The two stewardesses gave the relayed hand signals to the flight deck and I heard the number two engine begin to rotate. As the engine picked up speed, the low droning sound that it initially made had now increased in pitch to a more insistent howl. From previous experience I knew that when it made that noise, it was around the point where my colleague would be opening the fuel cock and introducing fuel into the engine. Just as I thought to myself 'any second now, she'll start,' there was an almighty whoosh and the whole area around me was brilliantly illuminated. I appeared to be standing in the middle of a huge volcanic eruption and as I felt a wave of heat hit me, I closed my eyes and grimly hung onto the cranking tool. We were experiencing a 'Flamer' (a Wet start). Basically, an excess amount of fuel had been introduced into the engine when the H. P. fuel valve was opened. The pilot has no control over how much fuel is passed through, because the fuel control unit should determine the amount. Occasionally, too much fuel can get through and, if there was already some unburnt fuel pooling in the combustion chambers at the time, the resultant light up as it ignites looks very dramatic. The sudden eruption of flames is usually brief in duration, but it certainly gets the attention of any onlookers, particularly if as in this case, it occurs at night. One thing is for sure, it certainly gets the attention of any poor bugger who happens to be standing underneath the engine at the time!

After a few seconds, I opened my eyes again to see that the flames had now subsided and I could hear that the engine had started. Just as I was thinking to myself 'thank goodness for that' I heard the engine shutting down again. Thoroughly confused, I headed back into the aircraft and made my way up to the flight deck. When I asked the captain why he had shut the engine down, he said that he had received a frantic radio call from another Dan Air aircraft that was parked next to us. They told him that they had been watching everything that was going on and when the engine torched, all they could see was my legs sticking out of a giant fireball. Needless to say, they shouted for him to shut the engine down and he quickly complied. Looking in a mirror on the flight deck door, I was relieved to see that my eyebrows were still intact and hadn't been singed off during the start attempt. The Captain then suggested we should have another go and held out the tool for me to take.

I told him that I'd had enough excitement for one night and that it was now his turn. With a laugh, he headed off to the back of the aircraft and I got ready to do my bit from the flight deck. I'm glad to say, the next engine start was perfectly normal and we set off on the flight home without further incident.

Chapter 18

Air Traffic Control Delays

T o say that the French air traffic controllers could be a militant bunch would be an understatement. Whenever there was a really busy period such as a Bank holiday or during the school summer holidays, you could pretty well guarantee that ATC in France would take industrial action, either in the form of a go-slow or alternatively an all out strike. They were usually after more money or more favourable working conditions and the French government would eventually give in to their demands, but not before a lot of chaos and frustration had been inflicted upon the airlines. As far as British air traffic was concerned, holidaymakers wishing to fly off to the sun had to head south through French airspace on the way to their destination. Instead of being able to depart on schedule, they would be informed that because of industrial action in France, their flight would be significantly delayed. At the end of their holiday, they would probably be faced with the same depressing news. Of course, when a flight is delayed, there is an inevitable knock-on effect for any subsequent flights that particular aircraft is scheduled to operate.

It's not only the French controllers who threw a spanner in the works of course and busy airports in other countries also imposed delays. In the summer months, Palma airport on the Spanish island of Majorca was one of the busiest airports in Europe. Having flown passengers into there from the U.K. we would typically be scheduled 45 minutes to get the passengers and their suitcases off, have the passenger cabin cleaned, the galleys restocked, the aircraft refuelled and the return passengers boarded with their suitcases loaded into the cargo holds. It was a well choreographed procedure and impressive to behold. As soon as you were ready you would call up ATC and request start clearance. Unfortunately, the reply often went something like this:

"Dan Air 4022, you are number 12 in the start sequence with 10 minutes between each start." In other words, you weren't going to be cleared to start for about 2 hours. Major delays at that airport became so commonplace that the company sent one of the operations controllers down there for the summer to try and improve things. He had a VHF radio installed in his Palma office so that our aircraft could call him up when inbound to the island. We were within radio range when overflying Barcelona on the Spanish mainland, so that was when we called him. If he replied with a coded message 'Early start request is required' we knew we should immediately call Palma ground on the radio. Using the flight number identifier for our return flight to London, we would ask for start up. Palma would ask us to confirm that we had all our passengers on board, the aircraft doors were closed and we were fully ready for start. We would reply 'Affirmative, we are fully ready.' If the controller had taken the trouble to look out of his window, the airport apron was rammed full of aircraft, many of them belonging to Dan Air. He would then say "Dan Air 4022, Standby. You are number 6 in the start sequence with 10 minutes between each start."

15 minutes later, we landed at Palma and 45 minutes after that (when we truly were ready for start) the controller would call us with the news "Dan Air 4022, you are cleared to start."

Chapter 19

From Hero To Zero

We had just flown our BAC 1-11 from the U.K. to the Spanish island of Minorca. The Captain had been the handling pilot for the outbound leg and so it was now my turn to be the handling pilot for the trip home. Consequently, I was walking around the outside of the aircraft carrying out my pre-flight external inspection. As I walked past the main landing gear bay, I heard a sudden whining noise and realised that the captain who was up in the flight deck, must have turned on an electrically driven hydraulic pump. To my alarm, I then saw fluid starting to pour out of the gear bay and pool onto the ground below. Clearly it was hydraulic fluid, so I ran to the nose of the aircraft and banged on the fuselage below the Captain's window. When his face appeared at the window I signalled for him to switch the pump off.

Minutes later, the Captain and I had our heads up in the main gear bay. The cause of the leak was immediately apparent. One of the hydraulic pipes had fractured. The split pipe had broken just short of the nut that coupled it to another hydraulic line. It looked like we were going to be stuck at the airport for some time. Needless to say, our traffic agent was hovering nearby and all he wanted to hear from us was the instruction that he could start boarding our passengers for the flight home. Of course that wasn't going to happen. Having told him to hold the passengers in the departure lounge for the time being, he then sent a Spanish engineer over to us in the vain hope that he could solve the problem.

The engineer arrived at our side and having looked at the hydraulic pipe for himself, he shrugged and gave us the international 'thumbs down' signal that indicates something is no good. He had his tool box with him, so I asked if I could use some of his tools. Having told the Captain that I might as well take the coupling nut off the broken pipe, I did exactly that. Once it was off, I used a hack saw to chop off the damaged end portion and noted that the remaining pipe could easily be moved so that it was butted up against the coupling point. The trouble was on course, the end of the pipe needed to be 'flared' so that the coupling nut, when slid to the end, would fasten the pipe securely in place.

An idea occurred to me so, with nothing to lose and everything to gain, I pressed a large Phillips screwdriver into the end of the pipe. With a few twists of the wrist, the pipe flared nicely. I offered it up to the joint and secured the coupling nut tight. The engineer even had some locking wire in his toolbox, so I used that to safety-lock the nut. Using some of the cans of hydraulic fluid we carried in the cargo hold, I refilled the system and then told the Captain that we needed to run the hydraulics to see if the pipe leaked. We agreed that running the flaps up and down a couple of times would put a load on the system and further test the integrity of the coupling. This we did and to my immense delight, not a single drop of hydraulic fluid appeared. The captain said to me, 'You are a bloody hero Bob. What a stroke of luck me having a first officer who was an engineer.' He then turned to the traffic agent and told him to board the passengers as quickly as possible. 'Come on Bob. We are going home and after we go off duty, I'm going to buy you a beer!'

We taxied out to the runway for departure and having received our takeoff clearance, I advanced the thrust levers and we roared off down the runway. I pulled back gently on the control column raising the nose of the aircraft and when the Captain called out 'Positive rate of climb' I asked him to bring the landing gear up. As the gear whined away in transit, I saw out of the corner of my eye, some warning lights flashing. Glancing across the flight deck I saw the hydraulic contents rapidly falling. Fortunately, we got the landing gear up and the flaps retracted before we lost all the fluid, so we were able to continue the flight to our destination (London Gatwick).

With our degraded hydraulics, we had to lower the landing gear by the alternate system and with normal wheel braking unserviceable we had to rely on the brake accumulators to slow us down after landing. Also we had no nose wheel steering so once we had turned off the runway onto the high speed turn off, we had to stop and wait for a tug to come out and tow us into the parking area. As a precaution prior to landing, we had asked ATC to have the emergency services standing by for our arrival, so we ended up being escorted to the parking area by a gaggle of fire department vehicles and rotating beacons flashing away all around us. The passengers thought we were heroes and gave us a rousing round of applause after landing. No doubt they dined out on the story of the exciting conclusion to their flight?

The engineers who met our aircraft thought it was all hilarious when we gave them the details. They did at least have the good grace to congratulate an embarrassed pilot (me) on getting the aircraft back to them so that some 'proper repairs' could be made.

Chapter 20

When Coffee Is Definitely Bad For You

We were cruising along in our BAC 1-11 at 31,000 feet. The autopilot was keeping us steady on our heading, the weather ahead looked clear and we were riding along in smooth air. Our flight deck was a warm happy place and we were enjoying the flight. Just then the door opened and one of the stewardesses entered carrying two cups of coffee. As she moved towards us, she suddenly let out a yelp as she tripped and fell forwards. As if in slow motion, the coffee flew out of the two cups towards us. Most of the hot liquid that had been in the Captain's cup splashed across his right shoulder and arm, causing him to cry out in pain and alarm. The liquid that had been in my cup didn't splash over me, but instead sprayed across the central radio pedestal to my left. The radios on this particular aircraft had their selected frequencies displayed by light emitting diodes. The brightness of the display automatically altered to suit the ambient light conditions. As I glanced down in horror at the coffee soaked radios, the frequency displays momentarily changed to 'full bright.' A couple of seconds later, one by one, each of the frequency displays went completely blank. The Captain hadn't noticed this for the time being, because he was clutching his coffee soaked right shoulder with his left hand as he simultaneously shouted out 'Jesus bloody Christ that's Hot!' The stewardesses stood perfectly still between us, her eyes like saucers and with an expression of horror on her face. I turned to her and said, 'Quick, soak a towel in cold water and bring it here for the captain and bring a load of dry cloths and towels as well.' She scurried away and returned a short while later with the towels.

The Captain grabbed the cold towel and wrapped it around his shoulder and arm and when I then said to him, 'We've got a big problem I'm afraid.' He looked across to see what I was doing. I was carefully mopping pools of coffee from around the upper face of our radios with the towels. It was immediately apparent that a lot of the liquid had seeped down through the gaps in and around each radio, so I pulled out a multi-tool that I carried in my flight bag. Selecting a screw driver blade from the tool, I started to release one of the radio's securing screws. The Captain asked 'Have you switched all the radios off? This was an understandable assumption on his behalf seeing that none of the frequency displays were illuminated. I glanced at him and said, 'I'm afraid not. They all seem to have failed when they became soaked in coffee.' On hearing this, the stewardess who was still standing behind us, burst into tears. She wailed 'Oh my God, what does that mean? What have I done?'

Having reassured her that she wasn't going to be responsible for some kind of air disaster, we continued with the mopping up process. We had two VHF communication radios, two VOR navigation receivers and two ADF navigation receivers. None of them were working. Unsure as to whether or not the transponder had been affected, I selected the code 7600 on it. If it was still working, that would inform ATC that we had suffered a radio failure. I had started out by removing the number one VHF comms box first in the hope of getting at least one communication radios working. As I withdrew it from the radio rack, coffee had poured out of it's electrical connection plug. This did not look good!

A short time later, we had managed to get one communication radio and one VOR navigation receiver to work again. Advising ATC of our degraded radio situation and with their much appreciated assistance (giving us radar steers and direct routing) we were able to continue to our destination.

Following this incident, the training department put out a notice requiring all cabin crew to place any Tea or Coffee cups into a dedicated container before entering the flight deck. This would retain the liquid inside the container rather than spraying it across the flight deck.

On the Airbus aircraft that I later flew, the pilot's coffee cup holder in the flight deck had been located in a really stupid place. With a cup slotted into the holder, all was well unless the aircraft encountered turbulence. Directly below the cup holder, was the pilot's navigation bag stowage. This was conveniently placed so that you could reach into the bag to retrieve books and documents. Needless to say, in turbulence, the coffee slopped and splashed out of the cup and straight into your bag. Soggy paperwork and an inch of coffee swirling around the bottom of their nav bag was a tell-tale sign that a pilot had encountered turbulence during their flight!

I clocked up 2,466 flying hours on the 1-11 and carried out 1,259 takeoffs and landings. During the course of completing those 1,259 flights, the occasional hiccup was bound to happen.

Five year's worth of 1-11 hiccups:

- Two in-flight engine shutdowns (not on the same flight I'm glad to say!).
- One engine failure on takeoff.
- Total loss of #2 hydraulic system and the loss of the emergency DC pump. This resulted in multiple system failures including the loss of some flight controls, loss of normal gear extension, loss of normal wheel braking and the loss of Nose-wheel steering.
- Gear unsafe indication when the landing gear was lowered. During a low flypast of the control tower at Gatwick, our engineers inspected the gear through binoculars and radioed to us that it looked to be normal. Subsequent landing was fine. Gear pins were inserted by the engineers and we were towed to the parking area.
- Diverted into Barcelona after we were informed by our Operations department that they had received a phone call saying there was a bomb on our aircraft. It was a hoax call.
- Starboard inner tyre blew on takeoff and large sections of the shredded tyre caused significant damage to starboard inner flap and number 2 engine intake. Emergency services attended for the subsequent landing, which was uneventful as the starboard outer tyre had remained inflated. Aircraft towed to the parking apron.
- Numerous air system failures over the years

(definitely the weakest system on the aircraft in terms of reliability.) When left with just one operative air system, the flight could be continued at a lower cruise altitude, but this resulted in higher fuel consumption and sometimes meant that we had to make an en route refuelling stop in order to get to our destination.

- Fractured wheel rim discovered during the walk around inspection in between flights. The crack was 6 inches long & resulted in a long flight delay waiting for a replacement wheel to be sourced & fitted.

- Temporarily lost all communications and navigation radios in the cruise. A stewardess tripped after walking into the flight deck. The two cups of coffee she had been carrying were tipped over the radio console and a few seconds later, one by one, all the radios died. We removed the radios, disconnected their individual wiring looms, and then dried them thoroughly with towels and cloths. After reconnecting them, we got one VHF Communications box and one VOR box to work again enabling us to complete the flight.

- During an ILS approach with the captain flying the aircraft, his flight director failed but without the associated warning flags appearing. I pointed out the disagreement between his flight director and mine. The ADF needles (that were tuned to the outer marker NDB) confirmed my flight director was correct and his was wrong. They showed that we were deviating left of the Localiser. The Captain carried out a go-around and because the weather was poor, with very low cloud and reduced visibility, he handed over the controls to me. We repositioned onto final approach and established on the ILS. After landing, the engineers confirmed that his flight director was indeed unserviceable AND the failure warning indicator wasn't working either.

- Number 1 Thrust reverser fault. In the cruise, the 'reverser unlocked' indication illuminated despite having forward thrust selected. After landing, the engineers locked out the reverser so that the engine was permanently fixed in forward thrust. This enabled us to fly the aircraft to Gatwick for remedial maintenance work.
- Radome damaged following an in-flight lightning strike. Two static wicks were also blown off the starboard wing where the lightning bolt had exited the airframe.

Chapter 21

You Can't Believe All That You Read

I t never ceases to amaze me how inaccurate many newspaper reports are when they cover the subject of aviation. As for comments you often see in various social media outlets? Let's just say that words fail me! Because aviation is a subject that I know something about, it really grates when I see glaring inaccuracies published about it. It makes me wonder just how accurate newspaper stories are on things that I know little about. We all realise that some news editors absolutely love a good disaster story. If they can come up with an attention-grabbing sensationalist headline, then copies of their publication will go flying off the shelves. An ill informed post on 'X' will soon go viral if it hints at a cover up or conspiracy by an airline or aircraft manufacturer. Rule number one seems to be 'Never let the truth get in the way of a good story.'

Many years ago, I came across a newspaper article that couldn't have got more facts wrong even if they had tried. The airline Dan Air was carrying out crew training in one of their de Havilland Comet aircraft at a U.K. airport. A number of their pilots who were already experienced on other aircraft types, were now converting onto the Comet. As part of that process, they were carrying out some takeoffs and landings under the watchful eye of a very experienced Comet training Captain. Once a trainee pilot had completed his quota of practice takeoffs and landings, he climbed out of his seat and was immediately replaced by the next trainee. This had been going on for some time but then, as the aircraft turned onto final approach once again and the pilot lowered the landing gear they saw that they had a problem. The indicators that show when the gear is down and securely locked, now showed that one of the gear legs wasn't locked down. The crew recycled the gear up and then down again, but the unsafe indication persisted. To cut a long story short, various procedures were carried out to fix the problem, but to no avail. A low flypast of the ATC tower enabled engineers on the ground to look at the landing gear through binoculars, but this revealed no issues and suggested all three gear legs were correctly down and locked. Armed with this information, the crew elected to come in for a landing, but as a precaution they requested to have the fire service standing by alongside the runway. They also confirmed that there were no passengers on board and that the flight deck crew were the sole occupants.

The aircraft landed safely shortly afterwards. It seemed that the 'gear unsafe' warning was merely a false indication. As a precaution, the crew elected to remain stationary on the runway until ground staff could insert gear down-lock safety pins into place. They were then able to proceed to the parking area. No drama. End of story. However, the next day, a newspaper reported the incident with the following headline:

119 passengers escape death in holiday jet drama.

The article that followed was totally inaccurate from start to finish. The only thing that the author did get right was the fact that Dan Air Comets were configured to carry 119 passengers. Of course, this particular aircraft didn't have any passengers on it at all, but the reporter wasn't going to let the truth get in the way of a good story!

I had another example of a local newspaper picking up on an aircraft incident, only this time I was directly involved. I was flying an Avro 748 turbo prop aircraft on a scheduled passenger service from Newcastle to Manchester. All was going to plan until we were on final approach to Manchester's runway and I selected the landing gear down. Instead of getting the expected 'three greens' (landing gear indicator lights) to signify that the three gear legs were safely locked down, we had two green lights and one red. The nose gear was locked okay, as was the starboard main gear. The port main gear was apparently not locked down. We tried various tricks to get it to lock, including manoeuvring the aircraft quite aggressively in pitch in the hope that the brief positive G forces would force the leg to lock. It was all to no avail, so with the emergency services standing by and passengers and crew fully briefed, we came in for a landing.

Fortunately, the gear unsafe indication proved to be a false warning, but after coming to a halt on the runway, we wanted to have the gear safety pins inserted before we taxied to the parking area. I opened the forward door and dropped the gear pins into our ground engineer's outstretched hands. As he started to insert the pins an airport policeman who had been standing next to him called up to me with the question "How many passengers have you got on board?" After I told him, he turned and hurried away.

I thought no more about it, until I read a local newspaper report the next day. The article was all about our little drama the day before. What caught my eye was the fact that it correctly quoted the number of passengers we had been carrying at the time. Obviously newspaper reporters rely on 'reliable sources' to provide them with the information they need for their stories. I have a sneaking suspicion that the reliable source in this particular case was the airport policeman who had spoken to me. His innocent enquiry about passenger numbers wasn't so innocent after all.

Chapter 22

Britain's First Female Airline Captain

During the time that I was working for the British airline Dan Air, I had the pleasure of flying with a remarkable lady called Yvonne Pope Sintes. Yvonne had an amazing career, having worked as an air stewardess, a flying instructor, an air traffic controller and then finally as a commercial airline pilot. In fact she was Britain's first female airline pilot, flying initially with Morton Air Services and then with Dan Air. Having flown as a first officer on the Dan Air Comet fleet, she was then promoted to Captain on their Avro 748 fleet. We first flew together on the 748 and then on the BAC1-11 jet when she later become a Captain on that fleet. As the first woman in Britain to have become a captain of a jet airliner, she was an inspiration to the very small number of women in the profession. As a trailblazer, Yvonne had needed to overcome a lot of resistance and prejudice along the way, but with stubborn determination she had overcome all the obstacles that had been laid in her path. Interestingly enough, she said that it was when she worked as an air traffic controller at Bournemouth and then Gatwick airports that she had encountered the greatest hostility amongst her colleagues. She was an excellent pilot and a pleasure to fly with, but one flight that we did together sticks in my memory and makes me smile.

We were operating a charter flight from London Gatwick to Spain in a BAC1-11. After we had been established in the cruise for a while, the number one stewardess came into the flight deck with a worried look on her face. She reported that one of the passengers was being very abusive and she suspected that he must have been drinking some of the duty free alcohol that he had purchased earlier. Other passengers who were sitting nearby had asked him to quieten down and stop using offensive language. Two members of the cabin crew had also asked him to behave himself, but he ignored them all and continued to be a pain in the backside. Armed with this information, I felt that it was down to me to go back into the passenger cabin and read him the riot act. Perhaps the sight of a man in uniform would make him pause for thought, particularly if I pointed out that if he didn't start behaving, we would land at the nearest airport and have him escorted off the plane by the police.

I turned to Yvonne and said 'Okay, I'll go back and see if I can get him to see reason.' Yvonne placed a hand on my arm and said 'No you won't. I'll go.' With that, she left her seat, put on her uniform jacket and hat and, marched out of the flight deck. Returning a few minutes later, she hung up her hat and jacket and sat back down in her seat. She looked across at me with a broad smile on her face and said, 'That wiped the smile off the silly bugger's face. When he looked up from his seat and saw me glaring down at him, he looked like he'd received an electric shock. Not sure if it was the shock of discovering that the captain is a woman, or my gently spoken suggestion that he surely didn't want me to have him arrested by the police. Either way, I left him with his mouth hanging open in stunned silence.' Yvonne giggled to herself and settled back into her seat. I just couldn't stop laughing.

In later years, it was decided that a pilot should not confront a passenger when the aircraft was in flight. Due to a marked increase in the number of air rage incidents, some of which ended in physical assault, airlines ruled that pilots should stay in the flight deck with the door securely locked. Whilst the prospect of leaving the cabin crew to their fate with a violent passenger didn't sit well with pilots, the reason for the ruling was fully understood. Having one of the pilots knocked unconscious by an irrational passenger really wasn't going to help the situation!

Consequently, the rule was that pilots stayed put in the flight deck & landed at the nearest suitable airport, radioing ahead for police and security officials to meet the aircraft on arrival.

Chapter 23

I Believe That Debris Might Belong To Us!

We were taxiing out towards the runway at Palma for our flight back to London Gatwick. We had landed about an hour before with a plane load of happy holiday makers and now we were taking another plane load back to the U.K. I had flown the aircraft out, so now it was Brian's turn to act as the handling pilot for the journey home. He lined the aircraft up at the start of the runway and having received our takeoff clearance from the tower controller, he advanced both thrust levers to bring the engines up to full takeoff power. About twenty seconds later, with the aircraft travelling fast and still accelerating, I called V1.

Before reaching this very critical speed, if an aircraft suffers a serious malfunction, there is still sufficient runway remaining to enable it to stop before reaching the end of the runway. After V1, that option is no longer available and the takeoff must be continued. Then, once the aircraft is airborne and climbing away safely, the pilots can initiate the appropriate actions to deal with the malfunction.

Having passed the V1 speed, we were now going too fast to stop and shortly afterwards, we reached the speed at which the nose of the aircraft should be raised in order to lift off the runway. As Brian gently eased back on his control column to rotate the aircraft, I felt a tremendous shudder pass through the airframe. Almost immediately, the nose of the aircraft began to swing to the right of the runway centreline, but Brian applied left rudder and prevented it from yawing any further.

'Whoa! Have we lost an engine?'

The question had come from Brian and I was thinking the same thing, but as I checked the engine instruments, nothing seemed to be wrong.

'Nope. No abnormal indications at all' was my reply. We continued climbing as we followed the profile of the standard instrument departure and everything seemed to be fine. None of our instruments suggested anything out of the ordinary had happened, but the vibration we had momentarily felt during the takeoff had been alarming.

Continuing our climb, we were aware of some radio chatter between the tower controller and another aircraft that had been on final approach for the runway we had just departed from. That aircraft had now landed and the pilot came onto the radio in a very agitated voice.

He shouted 'Tower, be advised there appears to be a lot of debris scatted along the runway. It looks like it might be large chunks of rubber from some tyres.'

There was no immediate response from the tower, so I replied "I do believe all that rubber debris might belong to us."

My next question was a pretty obvious one "Judging by what you can see, how bad does it look?"

The reply from the other aircraft was anything but encouraging.

"Judging by what we can see, I'd be surprised if you've got any tyres left!"

Fortunately, his assessment subsequently proved to be unduly pessimistic. That said, it was later discovered that we had been extremely lucky. One of the starboard main wheel tyres had exploded and completely detached from it's wheel rim. Large chunks of the flailing rubber had damaged but not deflated the adjoining tyre and wheel rim. Other sections of the tyre had struck the trailing edge flaps, denting and puncturing them in a couple of places. Even more significantly, what must have been a large section of the disintegrating tyre had been thrown backwards and hit the lip of the number two engine intake. The intake had been dented and had a rubber skid mark highlighting the point of impact. Obviously a large piece of the failed tyre had been propelled at high speed, hit the engine intake and was then deflected out past the engine. Had it instead been deflected into the engine, we would have suffered an engine failure to add to our problems.

At that stage, we were unaware of those details, but now knew that we had an abnormal situation on our hands when it came to landing the aircraft. We also realised that the affected gear may have caused damage within the wheel bay when we retracted the gear after takeoff. There are hydraulic reservoirs and pipe lines within that bay, so flailing chunks of rubber from a shredded tyre or jagged pieces of metal from a damaged wheel rim could really ruin our day.

Thankfully, as we carefully monitored all our instruments, with particular reference to the hydraulic systems, everything seemed to be okay. We decided to continue our journey towards Gatwick, whilst mentally selecting suitable airfields along our route that we could dive into should a problem arise.

We had plenty of time during the flight home to prepare ourselves for what lay ahead. We brought the cabin crew up to speed with regards to the current situation and ran through likely scenarios for the landing. We weren't going to brief the passengers for the time being, but instead intended to do that shortly before making our approach into Gatwick. There was no point in having the passengers worry about the situation for any longer than necessary, so the cabin crew carried on as normal as far as the passenger service was concerned. In the meantime, Brian and I discussed every eventuality and ran through all the emergency drills we were likely to be actioning.

Before we had signed off with the Palma controller on the radio, we had asked him to contact our company's operations department with any useful information regarding the debris we had left behind on his runway. Our hope was that they would be able to identify which tyre (or tyres) had failed and whether or not any wheel rim parts had been found and identified. When we eventually got within radio range of Gatwick, we contacted our company operations on their discreet radio frequency to see if there was any useful news from Palma. Unfortunately, there wasn't any so we were none the wiser. Next the passengers were given a full explanation over the public address system as to what had happened. The message was passed with lots of reassurances that they needn't worry (leave that to us!) and provided that they followed the cabin crew's instructions, everything would be fine. Next we alerted Air Traffic Control at Gatwick and asked them to have the emergency services called out and standing by for our arrival. With a final briefing between the two of us, Brian started the approach. We had decided that we needed to lower the landing gear much earlier than usual, to ensure that it did lock down properly. If the damaged tyre had fouled the locking mechanism in some way, we needed to know about it sooner rather than later.

Fortunately, when we did lower the gear, we got three green lights indicating that all three gear legs had locked down successfully. Our story ended happily. As it turned out, the other tyre on the starboard main gear leg, although slightly damaged, had remained inflated and held up okay. Brian had held the weight off that side of the aircraft for as long as possible after touchdown by inputting full left aileron. As the aircraft rolled to a halt on the high speed turnoff from the runway, we got a rapturous round of applause from our relieved passengers. As a precaution, a tug towed us to the parking apron at a slow pace with the emergency vehicles forming an impressive escort with their red beacons flashing away.

As a point of interest, the airline suffered two further high speed tyre failures soon after this incident. It was discovered that they had received a batch of defective tyres from the manufacturer. This turned out to be due to a fault in the tyre manufacturing process and needless to say, once identified, it was quickly rectified.

Chapter 24

Did He Just Say What I Think He Said?

We were flying in our BAC 1-11 at Flight level 330 (33,000 feet) beneath a star-filled sky. The visibility was excellent and the ride was smooth with very light winds. As is often the case at night, the radio frequency we were tuned to was pretty quiet with very little chatter between aircraft and air traffic control. I had seen the lights from the city of Bordeaux off to our right hand side a little while ago and the lights from the city of Toulouse were directly ahead of us. I glanced across at my colleague and saw that he was gazing up at the stars above us. I took another sip of my coffee and decided for the umpteenth time that this definitely beat working for a living.

I knew that the French controller who was looking after us for the time being, would soon be handing us over to a Barcelona controller as we approached Spanish airspace. Just then, and slightly sooner than I expected, the controller called us. As usual, he began his message with our airborne call sign in order to get our attention.

'Dan Air 4021 from Bordeaux control...' I replied

'Dan Air 4021, Go ahead.'

He then spoke very rapidly with a message that I really was not expecting. I looked across at Roger and asked 'Did he just say what I think he said?'

I called the controller and said 'Dan Air 4021, Please repeat your message.'

He replied 'Dan Air 4021, We have been informed by London that you have a bomb on board your aircraft. Please state your intentions.'

There followed some quick exchanges between the controller and I, during which we established that the information had originated from our company's operations department at Gatwick. The threat had been assessed as credible, with the recommendation that we should land at the nearest suitable airport.

Seconds later, we became very busy indeed. We changed our radio frequency to Barcelona control, declared an emergency and requested clearance to divert into Barcelona airport. Then we summoned the number one (senior cabin crew member) to the flight deck and quickly briefed her of the situation, told her how long before we expected to land (not long) and told her to brief her colleagues, secure the cabin for landing and advise us when that had all been done. We made a very brief announcement to the passengers on the P.A. telling them that we were having to land at Barcelona before continuing to our destination and that we were very busy at the moment, but would give them further information after landing.

The Barcelona controller told us that in view of our situation (possible bomb on board) they would have a 'follow me' vehicle direct us to a remote parking area well away from the airport terminal. We were fortunate that the BAC 1-11 has built-in air stairs at the forward and rear passenger doors, so our plan was for the cabin crew to extend those as soon as we gave the order over the P.A. Then, we would announce to the passengers that they had to leave all their belongings and vacate the aircraft as quickly as possible because we had been informed there was a bomb on board. We decided that if that announcement didn't make them get off the aircraft at a gallop, then nothing would. And that's exactly what we did.

When we turned off the runway after landing, a 'follow me' vehicle did appear and positioned itself in front of us, whereupon he drove at a furious pace as though he was trying to get away from us rather than leading us to our intended parking spot. I had already started the APU, so as soon as we came to a halt, the engines were shutdown and the order to vacate the aircraft was given over the P.A. The mention of a bomb certainly did the trick because I've never seen a passenger cabin empty so quickly. The cabin crew did a great job of leading the passengers a good distance away from the aircraft and, using a megaphone, got them into a reasonably well ordered group. Having checked that everybody was now off the aircraft, we joined our ragged band of refugees outside.

There was an impressive collection of vehicles parked some distance away from us. Some had blue flashing lights, some had red flashing lights, some had amber flashing lights. None of them appeared to want to move but instead just sat there. Lots of people were standing alongside the vehicles and they seemed to be frozen to the spot as well. A couple of them appeared to be observing us through binoculars. They watched us and we watched them. After a while, two men armed with machine guns slowly sauntered over to us and one said to me

'What is the emergency?' When I told him, he suddenly looked alarmed and spoke to his colleague in Spanish. His colleague looked even more alarmed and with that, they both turned around and scuttled away as fast as they could!

Eventually a bus arrived and transported our passengers to a departure lounge, whilst we were taken to a phone in order to contact our operations department at Gatwick. During that call, we discovered that there had been three phone calls made to the company that evening, each one identifying a particular flight (including ours) and stating that a bomb had been placed on those aircraft. The end result was that the company now had three aircraft sitting on the ground at various locations, each one having been forced to divert.

Armed with this information, we (the crew) then conducted a lengthy and meticulous search of the whole aircraft. This included having to unload well over a hundred suitcases from the baggage holds. Needless to say, none of the airport baggage handlers wanted to come anywhere near our aircraft until it had been thoroughly searched. In those days, the crew actually had a special checklist outlining every area of the aircraft that had to be inspected when checking for suspicious items. The passenger cabin, flight deck, galleys, toilets, storage cupboards and lockers, cargo holds and numerous maintenance access panels and compartments. We even had to carefully check inside the containers for the emergency escape slides at each doorway.

Security advisors had previously pointed out that a bomber could resort to placing a device inside a slide container, which would be triggered if the slide was deployed for an emergency evacuation of the passengers. A sobering thought indeed.

Once we had declared the aircraft itself was safe, the passengers were recalled and, having previously lined up all their suitcases outside the cargo holds, they each had to identify which case was theirs. Once it had been pointed out to us, we loaded it back into the cargo hold.

Thankfully, once they had all pointed to a suitcase, there were none left unclaimed. As you can imagine, by the end of this process we were both filthy dirty and thoroughly knackered. With everybody back on board, we started up and took off for our destination.

We were, of course, running late because of all that had happened and although we got the aircraft turned around as quickly as possible for the return flight to London, we were by then about three hours behind schedule. As the London bound passengers boarded the aircraft, many of them complained loudly to the cabin crew about the fact we were so late. I overheard one of them asking 'Well, what's your damned excuse for the delay?' The girl he had challenged merely smiled sweetly and said 'We are so sorry, sir. I'm afraid we experienced an operational problem on an earlier flight.' He stormed off down the cabin cursing loudly.

It would have been so much better if she had been able to say 'Sorry sir. We were busy searching for a bomb and it took longer than we expected. Unfortunately, we never did find it!'

Sometimes the girls just had to smile sweetly, even though they were seething inside. Likewise, I did a 'welcome aboard' greeting on the P.A. without making any reference to bomb threats or security scares. As for the clown who made the anonymous phone call that sparked off the security scare in the first place... words fail me!

Chapter 25

He's my husband, but I want nothing more to do with him

We had flown from London Gatwick to the Greek island of Heraklion. All our passengers had disembarked, the passenger cabin cleaned, the galleys restocked and the aircraft refuelled. The ramp agent had been told to bring out our returning passengers from the terminal building so we could quickly get them aboard and be on our way again. The air traffic controller had given us an approved takeoff time that meant we would be departing right on time. Things were looking good and the first officer and I were running through our pre-departure preparations and checks. I had seen out of my side window that our passengers had arrived at the foot of the forward stairs and had started boarding. Suddenly the flight deck door opened and the senior stewardess came in. She said, 'Looks like we've got a problem Bob.'

She went on to explain that the first few passengers to have arrived at the top of the steps had pointed down at the line of people who were waiting below and said 'I don't know which seat that man has been assigned, but I can assure you that I will be refusing to sit anywhere near him.'

When asked who they meant, they had pointed out a man who was being given a wide berth by everyone around him. Even from a distance it could be seen that he was drunk and looked to be in danger of falling over at any moment. I asked her where the ramp agent was, but she said that he was nowhere to be seen. Brilliant!

I left the flight deck and went to the forward passenger entrance door to take a look for myself. The man was at the bottom of the steps swaying around like a sailor in a rough sea and as he stumbled and tripped his way up towards me I couldn't believe that the airport staff in the departure lounge had been stupid enough to let him get this far. When he got to the doorway, I held my hand up and said

'Just a moment, sir. I'm afraid that I can't let you board the aircraft.'

He then waved his boarding pass at me and slurred out, 'I've got a ticket mate!'

The smell of alcohol on his breath was overwhelming and he continued to sway around alarmingly whilst trying to focus his bleary eyes on me. I explained that as he had clearly been drinking so much alcohol that he could barely stand, he would be a danger to himself and others, so was not going to be allowed to fly. He admitted that he'd had 'a little drink or two' but that he was fine.

This caused some passengers who were standing behind him to laugh out loud. One of them said 'You haven't stopped pouring alcohol down your neck for the past two weeks.'

This elicited a bout of swearing from our man, who then demanded to see the captain. When I informed him that I was the captain and that I was not going to permit him to fly, this was received with a blank look of incomprehension from him.

Knowing that I was going to have to find an airport official to escort the man safely away from the aircraft, I temporarily steered him into the forward galley so that all the passengers who had been patiently waiting behind him would be able to come aboard and find their seats. Just then, the first officer appeared and said that air traffic control had just called him on the radio with the warning that if we missed the approved takeoff time he had given us, we could expect a very significant delay trying to get a new one.

Because I was about to offload a passenger, I would now have to call the baggage handlers back to our aircraft and get them to search through all the suitcases in the cargo holds to find and remove his bag. This wasn't an act of kindness on my behalf to ensure the man had all his belongings with him. Instead it was a security precaution as we couldn't risk taking a bag on the flight if the bag's owner wasn't travelling with it. Unfortunately, I knew there was no way that his bag could be found and removed before our takeoff deadline had passed so it looked like we weren't going anywhere for quite some time.

Just then, a woman who had been standing in the aisle about halfway along the passenger cabin started walking towards me. She was holding a shoulder bag and when she reached me she turned to the drunk, looped the bag's strap over his head and said to him

'You will find your passport and some cash in that bag. I hope the police lock you up and throw the key away.'

I looked at the woman in amazement for a moment and then asked, 'Do you know this man?'

She replied, 'Yes he's my husband, but I want nothing more to do with him.'

Over the next couple of minutes, she explained that she was delighted I was about to chuck him off the aircraft and that she intended to remain on board and fly back to London with us. Better still, she said the suitcase down in our cargo hold was one they had both been sharing on the holiday. She had packed it for their journey home and she now intended to take it with her. With that, she turned to her husband and said, 'Just so you know, I shall be seeing my solicitor tomorrow to start divorce proceedings.'

She then turned on her heel and marched down the aisle towards her seat amidst a burst of applause and cheering from the other passengers.

By now, our ramp agent had finally made an appearance with two policemen in tow. I turned to them and asked them to escort our intoxicated passenger off the aircraft. I honestly don't think the man had a clue as to what was going on. He was so drunk that I doubt he even knew what his name was. Our cabin crew later discovered from some passengers who had been staying in the same hotel as the couple, that he had been a complete pain throughout the holiday and seemed to be permanently drunk. As soon as the police had taken him away, I ducked back into the flight deck and called the tower for start clearance. Despite everything, we were going to be leaving on time after all.

Chapter 26

Challenging, but Also Good Fun

L ike most people, I am all for an easy life, but I do need to inject a little bit of excitement into it now and then. Chucking myself out of an aircraft at twelve thousand feet whilst strapped to a tandem skydiver was something that I once needed to do for some reason. Paragliding off a hillside in Tenerife was another thing. Driving Formula Ford cars around a racing circuit as fast as I dared was yet another. I've also thrown aerobatic aircraft into some extreme manoeuvres whilst thoroughly enjoying the challenge of executing each manoeuvre successfully.

Whilst I've done all those things, I'm not a risk taker. I enjoy the buzz you get from running close to the ragged edge, but I've always known my limitations and ensured that I never exceed them. If I had a motto it would be, 'Know your limits and then push yourself to, but not beyond them.'

Working as an airline pilot, your priority is the safety of your passengers and crew. If you complete a flight and your passengers describe it as boring and uneventful, then you can probably pat yourself on the back for having done a good job. Sometimes, achieving that boring and uneventful rating is easy, but on other occasions, weather conditions, aircraft technical failures or unforeseen circumstances can make the trip far from boring. Those variations and uncertainties ensure that a pilot's job is kept interesting.

Airfields are categorised as being category A, B or C. Category A airfields are the 'no problem' ones. They have long paved runways with excellent lighting, approach and landing aids and licensed air traffic controllers to facilitate aircraft movements. There is no high terrain within the vicinity of the airfield and no unusual weather abnormalities such as wind shear, etc.

Category B airfields have some characteristics or features that are worthy of being highlighted and brought to the attention of pilots who are intending to operate into those airfields. These features can be outlined adequately in the form of a written brief and should be made available to a pilot as part of their preflight planning.

Category C airfields are deemed to be demanding in some way, either in terms of the runway, its approach procedures, its approach and landing aids (if any) and the surrounding terrain. The air traffic control facilities and airfield fire fighting facilities may also feature in the categorisation of the airfield. Specific weather related anomalies frequently feature at Category C airfields.

Because of their challenging nature, a written briefing is considered to be insufficient to prepare a pilot for their first visit to a Category C airfield. Consequently, they have to fly there under the supervision of a pilot who is already familiar with the place. Once cleared as being competent, their future visits can then be carried out unsupervised. Some airfields also require specific training in an approved flight simulator (for engine-out procedures, etc) before clearance to operate there.

As a training captain with a number of different airlines, I spent a lot of time flying in and out of Category C airfields over the years. Many of those trips were made in order to show another pilot how to safely operate in and out of there. I would point out the various things that could bite them during the approach and landing and then, provided that I was happy with the way they had handled the flight, I would clear them to operate there unsupervised for future visits.

Because Category C airfields are by their very nature more demanding, it was always satisfying to operate into one without the passengers even realising there was anything unusual about it.

Having said that, at some airports, if a passenger glanced out of their window during the approach to land, it is immediately apparent that the situation was far from normal. Funchal airport on the island of Madeira is like that. The original airport at F (Kai Tak) was most definitely like that.

The current airport at Hong Kong (Chek Lap Kok) is a modern and impressive airport that has been built on an island about fifteen miles west of Hong Kong's bustling city. It has two long parallel runways, sophisticated approach and landing aids, excellent air traffic control with radar coverage and a huge passenger terminal that puts most international airports to shame. However, before it opened in 1998, we used to operate into Hong Kong's original airport, Kai Tak. That was a very different, very interesting place indeed.

It's single runway (13/31) was 3,300 metres long, so plenty long enough. The runway was built out into Victoria harbour and so was surrounded by water to it's very edges. Not ideal but not a major problem. What was a problem however, was the terrain close to the airport. Because of the high ground, a straight in approach to runway 13 wasn't possible. Instead, you had to initially aim for a red and white chequerboard that had been erected on a hillside. You continued to descend towards this aiming point and just before reaching it, you had to bank the aircraft to the right, turning through about forty five degrees in order to line up on the runway which was a very short distance ahead. Throughout this manoeuvre you were skimming just above the buildings in downtown Kowloon and your passengers could look directly into people's living rooms as you whizzed past. You finally rolled the aircraft's wings level as you crossed the airport boundary fence and touched down seconds later. Needless to say, any passengers who hadn't flown into Kai Tak before were rather alarmed to look out of their windows and clearly see someone sitting in their living room watching television as we flew past them.

Chapter 27

What Happens When You Get the Computers Wet?

Early in 1994, I undertook a conversion course for a type rating on the Airbus A-320 aircraft. The initial part of the conversion was carried out in Miami at the Airbus training centre there. I was delighted to discover that one of the people on the course was Dave Rodgers. Dave and I had previously flown together many times on the Boeing 737 when we were employed by Dan Air.

Now we had both been offered temporary contracts with Air World, a new British charter airline that would be operating A-320 aircraft. Part of their deal with Airbus was that the aircraft manufacturer would type rate six captains and six first officers for each aircraft that the airline ordered. I was joining Air World as a captain and Dave as a first officer. Consequently, we were teamed up together as a crew for the duration of the course.

The time spent at the Miami training centre was pretty intense, with long sessions learning about the aircraft's various systems, interspersed with sessions

Skimming past the apartment buildings at Hong Kong's Kai Tak airport.

Kai Tak's runway juts out into Victoria Harbour.

Turning at the famous chequerboard at Kai Tak.

in the flight simulator to find out how to operate those systems and how the aircraft handled. Learning about the systems was achieved by spending long periods of Video Audio Computer Based Instruction (VACBI). This involved sitting in front of a computer monitor with headphones on and clicking a mouse to plough our way through each section of the syllabus. Diagrams and video clips were accompanied by an audio commentary that was delivered by the most monotonous and soporific voice I have ever heard.

For hour after hour we listened to the voice droning on, totally devoid of emotion or enthusiasm. Perhaps because it was feared that the voice could easily send us to sleep, the instruction was frequently punctuated with a series of quizzes. The questions had to be answered by clicking on one of the options on offer, only one of which was correct. If you answered all the questions correctly, you were allowed to proceed to the next section of the syllabus. Otherwise, you had to rerun the current section again. After many days of this torture, we were confronted with a final test covering the whole syllabus. As a training system, it worked well in terms of getting the message across and into our brains. That said, I can't help thinking that it would be even more efficient (and certainly less painful) if Airbus hired the actor Tom Hanks to provide the instructional commentary. His character 'Woody' in the film *Toy Story*, is so full of enthusiasm and humour that it would be guaranteed to maintain a student's attention throughout the course.

The part of the course that we enjoyed however, was flying the simulator. This was a sophisticated device with full three-axis motion and high resolution visual system.The instructor who had been assigned to look after Dave and I was a former Pan Am captain. His name was Fran Stull and he was a real character. He nicknamed Dave and I 'Lean, mean Dave and big, bad Bob.' We happily answered to those names and he kept us entertained and amused as he expertly guided us through the various stages of the course. Both Dave and I were amazed by how many computers were incorporated into the aircraft's various systems and how the method of operating the aircraft was totally biased towards using 'the automatics' (computers) as much as possible. At frequent intervals throughout our time together in the flight simulator, Dave had muttered the same question. Namely, 'What happens if you get these computers wet?' He joked that if he ever saw rain clouds ahead when flying an Airbus, he would want to land as soon as possible because computers and water don't mix well together. Some time later, that question that Dave kept asking suddenly became very relevant as I shall explain later. Over a period of four weeks, Dave and I 'flew' the simulator for a total of sixty five hours. During that time we covered every imaginable flight scenario, with Fran failing various systems one after another. It was a good old workout but thoroughly enjoyable.

Once our time in Miami was over, we travelled to Toulouse in southern France in order to undergo a flight test in a simulator there. The test was conducted by one of Airbus's type-rating examiners so Dave and I had to retune our ears from listening to Fran's American drawl and switch to the heavily accented English being spoken by our French examiner. All went well with the test, so our next task was to fly the aircraft itself for the first time. This was scheduled to be done at Cardiff airport in south Wales.

When the day finally arrived, I met with the base training captain who I was to fly with. We walked across the tarmac towards the A-320 that was parked some distance away waiting for us.

As we got closer to the aircraft I could see what appeared to be water pouring out from the back of it and commented on this fact to the training captain. He said, 'That will be water coming out of the domestic water overflow pipe.'

When we got a little closer, we could see that it was indeed water, but it wasn't coming out of the overflow outlet. It was pouring out of the rear passenger door which was open at the time.

Upon reaching the aircraft, we stared in amazement along with a number of engineers and airport ground staff. The passenger cabin appeared to be completely flooded with water along the full length of the central aisle. Water was even cascading out of the forward electronics bay.

I said 'I think we are about to find out what happens to the computers when they get wet.' Needless to say, our training flight was cancelled for the day. We later found out that one of the airport ground staff who had been tasked with the job of filling the domestic water tanks, had connected the hose from his servicing truck to the aircraft's coupling point. He then started the motor of his water pump and the filling process began. The system had a high level shut off switch so that when the tank was full, it would automatically close off the supply line. Knowing this, the guy decided to go off on a coffee break! Unfortunately for him, the high level shut off switch failed and the water kept on coming. The subsequent mopping up process was very extensive and took forever. Then hot air blowers were brought to the aircraft and trunking from those blowers was fed into the electronics bay and all the other sensitive and vulnerable areas around the aircraft. Drying everything out and getting it all functioning again proved to be quite a task. I blame Dave for raising the 'wet computer' question in the first place!

Chapter 28

Aviation Safety Over the Years

Everyone knows that flying as an airline passenger is very safe. It should, by all rights, feel scary, because that passenger will be flying six miles above the Earth's surface and streaking across the sky covering nine miles every minute. As they sit in their seat and gaze out of the window, they give little thought to the fact that the temperature just the other side of the glass is minus fifty degrees centigrade. Wearing just light clothing, they are perfectly comfortable in the temperature provided by the aircraft's air conditioning system. Also, the air outside their window is so rarified that if they were exposed to it, they would lose consciousness in no time at all. However, inside their warm and comfortable cocoon, the aircraft's pressurisation system allows them to breathe normally. Their biggest concern is probably what movie to select on the entertainment system or what drink to order from the cabin crew. Such is the tough life of a modern day air traveller.

Of course it wasn't always this way. During the span of my association with flying, I have seen enormous changes. The first aircraft that I flew on was not pressurised, so we were flying at a mere one and a half miles above the Earth and travelling at three miles a minute. The ride wasn't smooth because we weren't flying high above the clouds, but instead we were bumping our way through them. Because the cabin wasn't pressurised, the roar of the aircraft's engines was barely muffled and the noise was deafening. In fact we were given wads of cotton wool to stuff into our ears to lessen the din. Wrapped in a blanket because it was so cold, I didn't have a movie to watch, but instead my in flight entertainment was provided by gazing out of the window to see what I could spot in the darkness outside. More importantly though, the accident statistics in those days could be quite alarming. If we take for example the first airline that my father worked for, we see that between the years 1946 and 1949, they suffered ten crashes in just 29 months!

Years later, the first airline that I worked for had suffered five fatal crashes during their 39 year existence. That said, during the eighteen years that I was with them, they suffered four fatal crashes in just five years.

It is interesting to recall that when I first started flying commercially, insurance companies used to charge a higher premium for people who were employed as airline pilots. I think this was just a hangover from the 'bad old days of aviation' and they merely hadn't changed with the times.

When I applied for a life insurance policy, I filled in their application form which required me to state my occupation. My reply (airline pilot) jacked up the cost of the policy considerably. I was even penalised because of my occupation when I insured my car.

Their explanation for this was that they had statistics showing that airline pilots had been involved in road traffic accidents where it was suspected that they had fallen asleep at the wheel when driving home after a long flight. I remained unconvinced with that explanation, but at least they weren't trying to claim that pilots were driving their cars at 'aircraft speeds!' I should point out that these days, insurance companies no longer consider airline flying to be a high risk occupation.

If we look at today's aviation safety statistics, we can see just how incredibly safe it is as a form of transport. The airline EasyJet for example, began operations in 1995. Since that time, they have never suffered a fatal accident and today operate 330 aircraft, performing 1,800 flights a day. Truly impressive safety statistics by anyone's standards.

Throughout 2023, there were no fatal crashes worldwide involving scheduled passenger jets. There were two crashes involving propellor driven aircraft on scheduled domestic flights (one in Nepal and one in Brazil). These sadly resulted in a total of 86 deaths. During that same period, over 34 million flights were undertaken worldwide. The aviation fatal accident rate is less than one for every 15 million flights.

Despite these impressive statistics, some people are still frightened of flying. I think this is partly because every air accident receives extensive media coverage. Because an air accident often results in a large number of people losing their life, it sadly becomes newsworthy. That said, nervous flyers should consider the following: 148 people die every hour in road accidents around the world. That is over one and a quarter million deaths every year on the world's roads. Next time you are due to fly off somewhere on your holiday, perhaps you should bear in mind that the car journey to the airport could justifiably be considered the most dangerous part of your trip.

Chapter 29

Landing at the Wrong Airport

When they hear in the news that a passenger aircraft has landed at the wrong airport, members of the general public are understandably at a loss to understand how such a thing can happen. It is an extremely rare event, but it has happened a number of times.

Most international airports around the World have air traffic controllers using radar equipment to provide aircraft with guidance towards the airfield. Often they will instruct an aircraft to fly on a particular heading or series of headings that will eventually position it onto final approach to the runway. With the runway in sight, the pilots will then manoeuvre their aircraft to touchdown on that runway. In very bad weather, the radar controller's instructions will guide the aircraft onto the radio beam provided by an Instrument Landing System (ILS). This will then provide the pilot with indications for both horizontal and vertical guidance all the way down to the runway.

So far so good. However, problems can arise when

operating into an airfield that doesn't have radar facilities. Then a pilot will have to use whatever aids are available. In some cases, those aids might simply be landmarks or significant identifiable features in the vicinity of the airport.

Misidentifying expected features can lead to a condition known as 'confirmation bias.' For example, a pilot might have been told that his destination airfield is to the north of a small lake and that a road running from that lake actually leads directly to the airport. If he then sees a small lake appearing out of the mist and that lake has a road running from it, the visual picture confirms what he was expecting to see. Consequently, he follows the road knowing that it will lead him to the airport. Unfortunately, if the lake he has just overflown is in fact a different lake which is a couple of miles to the west of the correct one, and the road leading from it heads straight for an old disused runway... oops! Red faces and much embarrassment all around.

When the weather is fine and the visibility is good, it is tempting for a pilot to dispense with radar assistance and request a visual approach.They can then manoeuvre the aircraft visually to the runway and save some time. However, when a pilot is cleared for such an approach, they need to be absolutely sure that they are heading for the correct runway.

A classic example of this occurred in the U.K. one fine October day in 1960. A Pan Am Boeing 707 passenger aircraft was inbound to London Heathrow airport. It was a fine day with good visibility and the crew were expecting to catch sight of the runway very soon. There was a large gas container of the type often seen around towns and cities in those days and this particular one was located in the London district of Southall. Because of it's size, it could be seen from miles away and so had become a familiar landmark for pilots inbound to Heathrow airport.

By lining up on it, Heathrow's runway lay conveniently beyond the gas container. The Pan Am crew were aware of this and when they sighted a runway directly beyond the container, they advised the air traffic controller that they had Heathrow's runway in sight. The controller cleared them to land. A short while later they did land... at the wrong airport!

What the crew hadn't realised was that the gas container they had spotted was the wrong one. They had seen one that was located in South Harrow. Unfortunately for them, there is a runway visible beyond that container too, but it is at RAF Northolt airport. Worse still, the runway at Northolt is considerably shorter than the one at Heathrow so the crew really had to stand on the brakes after touchdown to avoid running off the end of it. The passengers were transferred to Heathrow by bus a short while later. After stripping the aircraft of as much weight as possible by removing seats and galley equipment, and with minimum fuel on board, the aircraft was later flown out of Northolt and positioned across to Heathrow just six miles away

Interestingly enough, confusion over the famous gas containers happened more than once. Vigilant air traffic controllers had alerted the pilots on those other occasions, but it was now realised that something had to be done about the problem. The solution was simple and caused great amusement to those in the know. They painted huge letters on the side of both containers. The gas holder in South Harrow which aligned with Northolt had NO written on it. The gas holder in Southall which aligned with Heathrow had LH written on it. Pilot's briefs highlighted this fact from then on. Both gas containers have since been dismantled and no longer exist. Perhaps it is just as well?

Chapter 30

What a Fantastic View You've Got

Years ago, we were allowed to invite passengers into the flight deck during the cruise so they could take a look at what we were up to at the sharp end. Sadly, because of increased terrorist activity and the resultant need for enhanced security measures, that practice is no longer permitted. It was something that was enjoyed by the passengers and the flight deck crews. Often an adult would appear at the door looking a bit self conscious whilst nudging a small child in ahead of them. The kids themselves however, couldn't wait to come in. As they took in the scene around them and scanned the various instrument panels, switches and controls, the look of sheer wonder on their faces always made me smile.

There were certain comments that you just knew you were going to hear. In the case of the Boeing 737 flight deck, the first comment from a passenger was usually 'They don't give you much room in here do they? It's much smaller than I expected!'

Of course we had some stock replies such as, 'They don't waste space on us because we didn't pay for our seats.' Alternatively, 'You're right. The Hollywood depiction of a flight deck is much bigger than this!'

The flight decks on the Boeing 757 and 767 and on the Airbuses were more generously proportioned, so the first comment from a visitor on one of those aircraft was usually, 'Wow! How on Earth do you know what all these switches and controls do? Do you really need them all?'

Once again the stock replies: 'Well I know what all these do' (sweeping your hand across a selection of them) 'And he knows what most of the others do' (pointing at your co-pilot). 'But neither of us is sure what those do' (pointing at a couple of random switches). It was vital that they laughed at our lame jokes otherwise their visit would be cut short.

Common questions were 'How high are we?' 'How fast are we going?' 'How do you know where we are?' 'What's the scariest flight you've ever had?' These questions would be punctuated by the person pointing at something to ask 'what's that for?' or 'How does that work?'

I was often impressed by some of the questions asked by very young kids. They're enquiring minds were clearly working overtime and they had no fear at all about looking silly or asking a dumb question (no such thing of course). They just came out with their question as soon as it popped into their heads and then followed it up with the next one.

Sometimes I enjoyed having a bit of harmless fun with small kids. On the Boeing 737, the central pedestal between the two pilots was almost waist high to a small toddler. At the very rear of the pedestal was a knob that increased or decreased the brightness of one of the overhead lights. I would point to it and ask the young toddler 'Would you like to turn the aircraft to the right?' Needless to say they would nod excitedly, so I'd tell them to twist the knob to the right and as they did so, I would sneakily turn the autopilot's heading selector twenty degrees to the right.

When I told the kid to look out of the window, they would see the aircraft gently banking to the right. After a couple of seconds I would tell them to twist the knob the other way and when I readjusted the heading selector again, the aircraft gently banked left onto it's original heading. The look of amazement and joy on the kid's face always made me smile. They were convinced that they had just turned the aircraft all by themselves and I wasn't going to tell them otherwise.

I'm convinced that many young kids grew up to become pilots because they once visited the flight deck and got hooked on the idea of sitting there themselves one day. Sadly, that method of recruitment is no longer an option.

One thing that everyone enjoyed was the view out of the generous flight deck windows. It is a sad fact, that in today's high flying aircraft, there is rarely a decent view out of a passenger's small window. From the flight deck though, the views were frequently spectacular. You could never tire of seeing the snow capped peaks of the Pyrenees or the Alps. Better still, the magnificent glaciers and icebergs when flying across Greenland. Also, the vast expanse and sheer desolation of northern Canada which seemed to go on forever as we flew westwards towards Vancouver. It was affectionately known as the GCSA, which stood for the Great Canadian Sod All.

Another view that seemed to go on forever could be seen when flying northwest across Australia from

Melbourne towards Indonesia. It showed the vast scale of that country in all it's glory. They were all incredible views in their own right, but sometimes the very best views came from above rather than down below.

Whenever I flew westbound across the North Atlantic, it was always in daylight, whereas eastbound flights were always at night. Sometimes those night flights were very special because of a natural phenomenon: the Aurora Borealis. Otherwise known as the northern lights, the display caused by charged solar particles following the earth's magnetic lines of force could be astonishing. The great swirling ribbons of light changing in colour and intensity were absolutely mesmerising. On a number of occasions I remember wishing that we could delay the onset of dawn and sunrise just so we could watch the light show for a little longer.

One November evening, I was operating a Virgin Atlantic scheduled service from London to Hong Kong. Because it was such a long flight, two pilots would operate the first and the end portions of the trip. For the middle portion, they would get their heads down for a few hours sleep whilst two more pilots took over control of the aircraft. We had been told prior to departure that the Leonid meteor shower was due to be at it's maximum intensity during the night and should produce an impressive sight. Our flight planned route took us north of the arctic circle as we made our way across Russian airspace. Shortly before we were due to be relieved by the other crew, the meteor shower started. Slowly at first, with a single 'shooting star' streaking across the black sky, followed by another around a minute later. Then the streaks of light increased in frequency and brilliance until it started to resemble a lavish public firework display. By now we had been joined by the other two pilots and the four of us stared out of the windows in amazement. We had turned the cockpit lighting and the instrument lighting down to a very low level so that it wouldn't distract us from the incredible sights outside the windows. At one point, one of my colleagues said that the sheer number of meteors that were showering into the upper atmosphere around us made him feel rather vulnerable in case we got hit by one. I replied that it looked like films I had seen of World War Two bombers flying through a barrage of anti-aircraft tracer fire. It certainly was an amazing sight and I didn't leave the flight deck to go on my break for quite some time. That was one show that was simply too good to miss.

Chapter 31

Autogyros Make You Smile

I took a flight in an open cockpit Gyrocopter and it was absolutely brilliant. The instructor was Jim Hughes and we flew from Rufforth, a former World War Two bomber airfield located to the south west of York. We flew for an hour, during which time Jim handed over the controls to me so I could get a feel for the machine. It was responsive, yet stable and most of all, it was bloody good fun! We then returned to the airfield and Jim proceeded to demonstrate the remarkable capabilities of a Gyrocopter. With vertical descents, split-arse turns and spot landings onto an area half the size of a tennis court, I was completely sold on Gyros. I knew I had to find out more.

Having been told that the CAA had decreed that a fixed wing pilot could undergo instruction and be awarded a Private Pilot's Licence (Gyroplanes) in as little as 25 hours total time, I decided that was what I was going to do. My infinitely patient and understanding wife Sara listened as I passed on this news and then gave me a brief but unmistakeable 'When are you going to grow up' look. I immediately recognised this to mean that she thought it was a brilliant idea and I should get started as soon as possible.

On the first of September 2015, Jim Hughes and I got airborne in his MTO Sport for my first Gyrocopter flying lesson. When we got back, I was grinning from ear to ear. I knew this was going to be a lot of fun.

The aircraft that I learned to fly was the AutoGyro MTO Sport. AutoGyro is a German company and their workmanship and standard of engineering is excellent. The gyro is powered by the very popular Rotax engine and is tuned to run on regular unleaded fuel. Cruising at 70 knots, it uses around 15 litres per hour. The aircraft is fitted with a pre-rotator so before takeoff, the engine can spin the main rotor up to about 80% of the rotation speed required to fly. The pre-rotator is then disengaged and opening up the power on the Rotax engine moves the aircraft forward. As it moves forward, the airflow that passes through the main rotor increases the rotation speed by another 20% which gives sufficient lift for takeoff. The gyro has a very short takeoff roll of about 150 metres in still air and much less in a significant headwind. Once airborne, the airflow through the main rotor keeps it 'autorotating' in much the same way that a Sycamore seed spins as it floats to the ground. This makes the Gyrocopter very safe because if the engine stops in flight, the main rotor will continue to turn, enabling the pilot to make a controlled descent, culminating in a smooth landing with negligible ground roll. A ground roll of just 15 metres is typical, so you really can put it down onto a tiny space in an emergency. The aircraft is very manoeuvrable and responsive, but also extremely stable and it rides through turbulence beautifully. I really enjoyed exploring it's capabilities.

It was a fairly long drive to Rufforth from my home, so after I'd spent a few days driving back and forth to the airfield, I decided to book myself into a bed and breakfast place in the village of Rufforth for a few nights. I was then able to put in a full day's flying each day without having to worry about driving home afterwards. Besides which, there was nothing better than a few hours flying followed by a couple of welcome pints in the village pub.

After completing exactly twenty five hours of flying, including nine hours solo, I booked my GFT (General Flying Test). The flight examiner was Phil Harwood, a highly experienced and very enthusiastic Gyroplane pilot. He gave me a good 'workout' at the end of which I was awarded a pass. I was now the proud holder of a Private Pilot's Licence (Gyroplanes.)

What I loved about flying gyros was the fact that it took you back to the basics. It was good old stick and rudder flying and it put me in mind of those early days at Blackbushe airfield when I was flying the old Piper J-3 Cub. In fact the cruising speed of the MTO Sport was about the same as the J-3 Cub. What I also liked about flying from Rufforth was the relaxed do-it-yourself way of operating there. You would open up the hangar and manhandle your aircraft out. This could be a very delicate process because lots of aircraft were housed in there so you had to be careful not to cause 'hangar rash' by dinging one of them. I kept a couple of 20 litre Jerry cans in the boot of my car and would fill these with unleaded fuel on my way to the airfield. Using a funnel, I decanted this into the tanks of the gyro. I then did a preflight inspection of the aircraft and topped up the engine oil if necessary.

After a pre-departure pee behind the hangar, I would zip up my flying suit and climb aboard. There was no air traffic control at the airfield, so you just started up the engine and taxied out to the runway. No load sheet to complete, no scheduled departure time to achieve, no approved takeoff time to worry about. Just go when you are ready.

After warming the engine, checking the magnetos for correct operation, checking the flight controls and running through the pre-takeoff checks, you looked to see if there was anybody on final approach to the runway. If it was clear, you lined up and took off. Fantastic! What could be better?

Because a Gyroplane needs so little space to takeoff and land, when you want to head off in search of a new destination, you aren't confined to using just airfields. The smallest of grass runways or farm strips will be perfectly adequate for your needs. Consequently, there are literally hundreds of places to choose from in the U.K.

A company called AFE produce an excellent publication called U.K. VFR flight guide. This lists the various destinations, along with a diagram of the runway and surrounding area. It details operating hours, air to ground radio frequencies and any special procedures for operating in and out of there. I bought the guide and studied the huge number of options. It was time for me to go exploring.

After a brief study of the VFR flight guide, I immediately found somewhere that I wanted to fly to. There is a grass airstrip just to the south of RAF Coningsby in Lincolnshire. The reason I was keen to land there is because it's called New York. After a further study of the guide, things got even better. When planning my flights, I always selected a suitable alternate airfield in case something cropped up to prevent me from being able to land at the intended destination. I was delighted to discover an airfield that was just perfect for my New York trip, the reason being it was called Boston. So, it was that I set off for New York knowing that in the event of having to divert, I could fly to Boston.

RAF Coningsby is home to three front line Eurofighter Typhoon squadrons and the Battle of Britain Memorial Flight. New York is actually inside Coningsby's ATZ and is just one and a half miles south of it's runway. I was approaching from the north and contacted Coningsby approach on my radio to see if I could get clearance to overfly their airfield. To my delight, the controller told me I was cleared to proceed provided that I didn't exceed an altitude of five hundred feet as I crossed the airfield. I told him that would be no problem and shortly after, I flew over some Typhoon fighters that were parked in a line. A couple of pilots were sitting on the wing of one of the aircraft and they looked up with a startled expression as I flew over them. I gave them a friendly wave and they all waved back. Buzzing a front line RAF airfield at 500 feet was definitely a moment to savour.

A few minutes later I landed at New York and met the owner of the place who was working on an aircraft in his hangar. After a cup of coffee from the thermos flask I brought with me, we spent some time chatting together and then, having put the world to rights, I bade him farewell and took off again. What a lovely way to pass a few hours on a fine sunny day. Needless to say, from that day onwards, if ever someone asked me how far you can fly in a Gyrocopter, I used to casually say that I once flew one to New York.

Shortly before my New York trip, I had been talking to my sister-in-law and she said she would love to take a flight in a Gyrocopter. She lives near a town called Repton in Derbyshire, so I took a look in my trusty VFR flight guide to see if there was an airfield reasonably close to her home. I discovered that Derby airfield was just a few minutes by car from her house, so we arranged a day for me to fly there in order to pick her up and take her for a flight around the local area. Derby is a very nice little airfield offering three grass runways, a cafe and a bunch of friendly fellow aviators.

When I landed there, my sister-in-law Cal had already arrived by car a short while before. We soon set off for our flight and a few minutes later flew over her house in Repton. She had told her neighbours that we would be coming and much to our delight, they had stationed themselves out in their garden. They waved excitedly and took some photos of us as we flew overhead. Cal's husband Chris had an office a short distance from their home, so that was our next port of call. After a couple of orbits of his office we set off for a bit of sightseeing around the local area. The last time Cal and I had flown together, I was flying a Dan Air Boeing 737 and she was a member of the cabin crew. At that time, my wife Sara, her older sister Cal and her younger sister Jo were all air stewardesses with Dan Air. I used to joke that even when I went to work, I couldn't get away from the family because at least one of them would probably be on my crew. Now, all these years later, Cal and I had flown together again. The amusing thing is, at the time of our gyro flight, she was employed as cabin crew with British Airways on the Boeing 747. The difference between the two aircraft could hardly have been any greater!

After my sister-in-law started the ball rolling by flying with me in a gyro, her husband Chris quickly followed suit and we went on a flight together from Rufforth. On that same day, I also took my daughter Phoebe for a flight. Her request to fly in a gyro made me a little uneasy, because I knew that she even felt slightly nervous about flying in large passenger jets. This was something that she had kept from me for a long time because she somehow felt that the daughter of an airline pilot shouldn't be afraid of flying. Now, she was proposing to climb into an open cockpit Gyroplane and take to the skies in a machine that exposed her to the elements in a way that an airliner never could. Was this a good idea?

There was only one way to find out. To cut a long story short, she thoroughly enjoyed it. In fact, to such an extent that we ended up doing some steep turns and quite sporty manoeuvres much to her amusement. Amazingly, her fear of flying had been cured by taking to the skies in a very small, very basic, open cockpit Gyrocopter.

My former gyro instructor, Jim Hughes had started working for Rotorsport out of Wolverhampton airport at this time. Rotorsport are the main distributor for Autogyro in the U.K. and so have a number of their different models at their hangar. The MTO Sport model that I usually flew, is a tandem seat open cockpit aircraft. The company also produces the Calidus, which is a tandem seat machine with an enclosed cockpit. In addition to this, they produce the Cavalon which is a side by side two seater model with an enclosed cockpit.

I decided to give that one a try, so Jim and I took to the air in the Cavalon so that I could do some 'differences' training in it. It is an impressive machine and I enjoyed flying it. It's sleek looking streamlined cabin protects you from the elements and it cruises a little faster than the MTO Sport. You have the luxury of a cabin heater to keep you warm whatever the weather and the Pro variant even has a sophisticated glass cockpit and is cleared for night flying. However for me, the attraction of Gyroplanes is the pure joy of an open cockpit. The MTO Sport is like a flying motorbike and all the more fun because of it. It is also a lot more agile and responsive than the Cavalon, so it remained my firm favourite.

To get to the airfields at Rufforth or Wolverhampton involved a fairly long car journey from my home, so I was looking for somewhere nearer. Whilst at Rufforth one day, I met Phil Robinson who is a helicopter instructor. He owns the Flight Academy at City airport (Manchester Barton) and he told me that he was going to be basing a MTO Sport Gyrocopter there. His plan was to make it available for flight instruction or for personal hire. This was music to my ears as Barton airport is only a twenty minute drive from my home. It wasn't long before I was flying in and out of Barton on a regular basis.

The Air Traffic Controllers at nearby Manchester airport didn't usually have to deal with General Aviation traffic out of Barton, but if you asked them nicely they could be very accommodating. One day I took my son Joe up for a flight in the gyro. Joe is a lifelong fan of MCFC (Manchester City Football Club) and before we took off from Barton I phoned the controllers at Manchester and told them that I wanted to fly over Man City's Etihad stadium and stooge overhead their Football academy complex and training grounds to take some photos. They told me to give them a call on the radio once we were

197

airborne and they would 'see what they could do.' Sure enough, they were happy to let us do exactly as I had asked and so Joe and I were soon enjoying a bird's eye view of the Man City complex. Once we'd had our fill, I thanked the controller and we set off for a sightseeing tour further afield. Needless to say, moments of co-operation and assistance like that are always very much appreciated.

In the late eighties, my parents had sold their longtime home in Surrey and had moved to Abergavenny in South Wales. When visiting them there, I became very familiar with the drive down the M6, M5 and M50 motorways and after passing through Ross-on-Wye and Monmouth, the final run to Abergavenny was via the A40. Depending on traffic conditions, it could be quite a long drive and so, imagine my surprise when I looked at my VFR flight guide one day and discovered that there was an airfield just two nautical miles south east of Abergavenny. By now, both my parents had passed away, but I decided to make another trip to Abergavenny, this time by air.

In May 2017, I flew from Barton down to South Wales. Rather than flying directly to the airfield, instead I made for Llanfoist on the outskirts of the town of Abergavenny. Both my parents are buried in a small cemetery there. It is a quiet spot just to the south of the river Usk and nestles close to a hill that is popular with hang glider pilots. I slowly circled the cemetery and gave my parents a salute from above, before heading off directly to Abergavenny airfield. I had previously wondered why I didn't know the airfield existed, despite repeated visits to my Parent's home over the years. The reason became apparent when I arrived overhead. Although the grass runway

The AutoGyro MTO Sport.

runs parallel and close to the A40, it is completely screened behind a long line of tall trees.

Having landed, I parked the gyro and was met by Frank Cavaciuti the operator and owner of the airfield. He made me a cup of coffee and we sat down together for a chat. Frank had just returned from Europe in his light aircraft and we talked about that for a while.

There were two aircraft parked in his hangar and he happened to mention that one of them was owned by a guy who was a Boeing 747 Captain with Virgin Atlantic. I told Frank that when I was flying for Virgin, I knew a pilot who lived somewhere in the Abergavenny area who had built his own house. Frank smiled and said that we were talking about the same person. Once again, I was reminded just what a small world it can be, particularly when it comes to aviation.

The ability to drop into interesting private farm

strips and small airfields was one of the things I liked most about flying the Gyrocopters. That and the do it yourself, come and go as you please nature of the flying really appealed to me. It is of course vital to maintain a professional approach when it comes to flying and that is just as true when flying solo in a small aircraft as it is when flying a commercial jet with hundreds of passengers sitting behind you. The old joke that the pilot is always the first person to arrive at the scene of a crash is very true. Consequently, it is in the pilot's best interest to ensure they do a good job. When flying single engine aircraft, I always made sure that I regularly practiced forced landings by simulating an engine failure and then setting the aircraft up for a glide approach and landing. In the gyro, I regularly practiced forced landings, vertical descents and various advanced manoeuvres to keep my hand in. Good practice and also really good fun.

In June and early July of 2018, we experienced some fabulous weather in the U.K. For day after day, we enjoyed sunshine, cloudless blue skies and terrific visibility. Perfect weather for flying in an open cockpit Gyroplane. I decided that I wanted to fly up to Scotland and tour around for a couple or three days, landing at various places and generally enjoying myself. Part of the fun with regards to cross country flying, is planning your route and working out details such as the availability of fuel, overnight parking facilities for the aircraft, what accommodation is available and so on. I got stuck in and mapped out my Scottish adventure.

When I had been training for my Gyro licence at Rufforth, there had been another guy there by the name of Will Roomes who was also undergoing training. He owned his own aircraft, an MTO Sport and had the same instructor as me (Jim Hughes). Once he got his PPL, Will went on to get his instructor's rating and then he moved up to Inverness with his family. His original plan had been to set himself up at Inverness airport and offer trial flights and flying lessons in his Gyro. As things turned out, he ended up going into partnership with a friend and taking over a flying school that was already established at Inverness. The school (Highland Aviation) already operated some fixed wing aircraft, but after Will arrived on the scene, they were able to offer Gyroplane instruction as well. I knew that I would need to have somewhere to keep my Gyro overnight if I flew to the Scottish Highlands, so I contacted Will to see if he could help. Will is such a generous guy and he said that I could keep my Gyro in the flying school's hangar and that I was welcome to stay at his home for the night. What a star!

I contacted the guys at Barton and booked Zulu X-ray for a three day trip. However, even the best laid plans can go wrong and that is exactly what happened next. The Flight Academy at Barton phoned me to say that the radio in the Gyro had packed up and had been sent off for repair. In desperation, I phoned Jim Hughes in Wolverhampton and asked him if one of his Gyros was available for hire for a few days and he confirmed that one of them would be free the following day. I told him that I wanted to book it and that I would pick it up from the Rotorsport hangar in the morning. I then booked a bed and breakfast place near Wolverhampton airport, hopped into my car and drove down there. The Scottish trip was back on.

I had planned to make the journey in a series of reasonably short sectors for two reasons. Firstly, I liked visiting airfields I hadn't been to before and enjoyed having a Coffee and a chat to the people that I met there. Secondly, there is nothing more uncomfortable than wanting to take a pee, but being unable to do so. Therefore, choosing stops that are well within your bladder's endurance limit makes a lot of sense.

The first leg of my journey was a one hour and fifty minute flight to Sherburn-in-Elmet. It was nice to see how busy the place was, with lots of aircraft coming and going throughout the short time I was there. I stayed long enough to top the aircraft up with fuel, enjoy a nice cup of Coffee in the café and then have a quick pee before taking off again.

My next stop was Eshott, to the north of Newcastle, which was a two hour flight away. Another aircraft refuel and Pilot defuel and I was on my way again.

Next stop was to be Scone airfield, near the city of Perth. On route to Scone, I made a point of overflying the former World War Two airfield East Fortune, which is located to the East of Edinburgh. It is now the location of Scotland's National museum of flight. Many exhibits are housed within the hangars there, including a Concorde. However, I was keen to get a bird's eye view of two aircraft that are parked out in the open. One is an Avro Vulcan and the other is a de Havilland Comet 4C that had formerly been owned by Dan Air. The airline had handed it over to the museum once it came to the end of it's operational life, since which time it had remained on display in the smart Dan Air paint scheme. Sure enough, I had a great view of the aircraft as I flew directly overhead. I then crossed the Firth of Forth and coasted in over Leven before continuing directly to Scone. The flight to Scone took just one hour and twenty five minutes and as I cleared the runway and taxied towards the

My sister-in-law Cal and I flying over her house
(May 2016).

apron, the Tower controller spoke to me on the radio and asked if I was staying overnight or just refuelling before departing again. I replied that I was just going to refuel and then head off again, at which point he asked 'Have you been to Scone before and are you familiar where the fuel pumps are? I could actually see the fuel pumps in the distance but couldn't resist replying 'Yes I have been to Scone before, but it was actually forty five years ago, when I trained here for my Commercial Pilot's Licence.' There was a pause before the Tower controller came back on the radio. 'Well, nothing has changed... except the price of the fuel.'

It felt strange to be back at the airfield that had been my home for a year. Much of it did appear to be largely unchanged and familiar and I took a look inside the very large hangar that had housed the Cessna 150s and Cessna 310s that I had flown back in 1973. Air

Service Training doesn't do any Commercial Pilot training anymore, but they do still have a presence at Scone, training aircraft engineers. The hangar was full of many types of General Aviation aircraft, but as I came out of the hangar, a very interesting aircraft taxied in and shut down near my gyro. It was a very smart looking 80% scale replica of a Spitfire. I briefly spoke to the owner who was sitting in the cockpit and he told me that it was actually up for sale. After a fleeting daydream of actually owning his Spitfire, I decided to walk away whilst I was still capable of rational thought. It was time to head to Inverness.

My original plan had been to fly over the Cairngorm mountains on a direct track to my destination, however the sky had now clouded over and the base of the overcast looked to be too low to enable me to take that route. I went into the building that had formerly been the Operations room back in the AST days and started checking on the weather reports for Aberdeen and Inverness. It soon became apparent that the weather was deteriorating, but that Aberdeen and Inverness were both still okay. Because of the cloud buildups, I was going to have to route Northwards from Scone, keeping to the East of the mountains, whilst also avoiding Aberdeen's controlled airspace. I planned to head up towards a small town called Keith, before turning to the West towards Inverness.

I hadn't gone very far north of Scone before it became apparent that the weather had deteriorated still further and I was having to deviate from my planned track in order to keep clear of some isolated but significant rain showers. I was talking to Scottish ATC on the radio and keeping them informed of my intentions and updating them with any changes. I was also having to descend to a lower altitude in order to remain below the cloud base. It was starting to get rather interesting and the Scottish Controller asked me to confirm that I was still in VMC (Visual Meteorological Conditions) with good contact with the terrain. Clearly he was getting a little uneasy on my behalf.

I soon ended up 'scud-running' for about twenty minutes, with the visibility down to about 1,500 metres in rain, solid cloud not far above me and the ground not far below me. With no blind flying instruments whatsoever, losing visual reference with the ground would have been disastrous, so I was keeping an eye out for any open ground to land on. I then became very busy weaving my way around a number of wind turbines that appeared out of the mist. Grateful for the Gyro's agility and manoeuvrability, I cursed myself for making the classic 'Rookie' mistake of continuing a flight in weather conditions that were quite obviously going from bad to worse. Fortunately, a few minutes later, the visibility improved and the cloud base lifted a little, so I was able to continue without further difficulty.

I landed at Inverness and taxied up to the Highland Aviation building. Will Roomes was there to greet me and he helped me to put the Gyro to bed for the night in his hangar. We then drove to a nearby Pub for a meal and a very welcome pint of beer.

I used to use the excellent SkyDemon programme on my iPad for flight planning and GPS navigation when flying the Gyro. The shot overleaf is a recording of part of my flight from Scone to Inverness. The magenta line shows my originally planned track, whilst the blue line shows the track I actually followed because of having to deviate around heavy

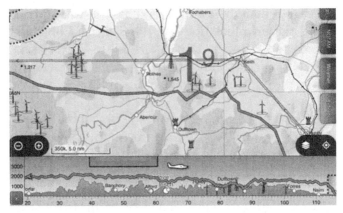

rain showers. The elevation view at the lower part of the picture shows how interesting things got to the North East of Dufftown when I was weaving around the wind turbines.

The original plan for my trip to Scotland was that I would spend the night at Will's place and then fly from Inverness to Wick, John O' Groats airport. From there, to the Orkney isles for a landing at Kirkwall. Once on the Island, there was another place that I definitely wanted to fly to. In keeping with my amusement at having New York, Boston and Melbourne in my logbook, there is a disused airfield on Orkney that used to be a Royal Naval Air Station. Although it is no longer in use, I childishly wanted to at least fly to the place because of it's name. It's a place called Twatt. (For anybody who doesn't believe me, it's location is N5905.17, W00317.02.)

For my return southwards, I had planned and tentatively received prior permission for visiting a couple of airfields on the Western isles. From Kirkwall, I was going to Stornaway and then to Campbeltown and then Carlisle. It was an adventure that I was really looking forward to and after a good night's sleep at Will's house, I pulled back the

Zulu X-ray in the hangar at Barton airfield.

bedroom curtains to take my first look at the day's weather. It was NOT what I was hoping for.

The whole place was shrouded in fog and a fine drizzle was falling. The visibility was terrible. I went on line and checked the weather in all the areas of interest. It was immediately obvious that I wouldn't be flying anywhere.

With flying out of the question, Will drove me out for a visit to the very impressive Fort George garrison that sits guarding the mouth of the Moray Firth. Then it was back to Will's place where his family very kindly entertained me and put me up for another night.

The next day, the weather was still not good and it was obvious that my original flight plans had to be ditched. The whole of the Western side of the country was experiencing really bad weather and it wasn't going to improve in a hurry. I decided that I had to try and get the gyro back down to Wolverhampton by whatever route was workable in terms of weather. I did some more planning and finally, having thanked Will for all his help and hospitality, I set off for the flight home.

I arrived overhead Wolverhampton airport (via Scone and Rufforth) several hours later and just 10 minutes before sunset. The Tower was closed and everyone had gone home, so it was a case of noting the wind direction and choosing a runway for myself. After landing, I put the gyro into the hangar, climbed into my car and headed for home.

On the way home I had a thought that made me smile. I had just done six and a half hours of hand flying, during which I had dodged and weaved my way around numerous areas of shower activity. I'd done three takeoffs and landings and refuelled the aircraft twice. And I had thoroughly enjoyed every moment. What made me smile was the thought of turning up for work when I was with the airlines and the operations department saying to me 'I'm afraid that your aircraft has an unserviceable autopilot, so we need you to hand fly it for six and a half hours. Is that okay with you?'

My reply of course would have been unprintable, yet here I was flying purely for pleasure and perfectly happy to clock up six and a half hours of hand flying. I think that just proves that flying Gyroplanes really is 'fun flying.'

As it turned out, I didn't fly Gyroplanes for very much longer after that. In fact I did just six more flights, the last one being on the ninth of October 2018. I flew G-CFZX from Barton to Wolverhampton and after a brief spell on the ground there, I flew back to Barton.

Although I didn't know it at the time, when I touched down at Barton that day, it would be the last time that I

Zulu X-ray at Sleap airfield in Shrewsbury.

landed an aircraft. I had begun suffering with persistent fatigue and it also seemed as though I kept coming down with a series of colds and infections. Feeling under the weather and more or less permanently tired, in November 2018 I went to see my Doctor and he made an urgent appointment for me at our local hospital. Over the weeks that followed, I had a total of three biopsies and was finally diagnosed with stage three Hodgkin's Lymphoma.

This is a type of Cancer that affects the Lymphatic system, which is part of the body's immune system. There followed a full body PET scan, further blood tests and then my consultant outlined a treatment plan. Over the next three months, I underwent Chemotherapy at the excellent Cancer unit at Macclesfield hospital. A few weeks after completing the Chemo course, I was given another full body PET scan at Christie's hospital, following which I'm delighted to say, I was told that I was free of Cancer and in remission. From the initial diagnosis to the 'all clear' diagnosis had taken seven long months, but thanks to the excellent team who had cared for me during that period, the final outcome was good.

With a clean bill of health, I considered the idea of revalidating my Pilot's licence and taking to the skies again. Obviously I would have to undergo some refresher training and then get a flight examiner to give me a check ride in order to renew the license. I was perfectly prepared to do that, but after some careful consideration I decided that it was probably a good time to hang up my flying goggles for good.

21,000 accident-free flying hours and lots of happy memories. That seemed like a good time to quit.